# ESSAYS IN
# CHRISTIAN PHILOSOPHY

# ESSAYS IN
# CHRISTIAN PHILOSOPHY

BY

## LEONARD HODGSON
M.A., Hon. D.C.L.

PROFESSOR OF CHRISTIAN APOLOGETICS IN THE GENERAL
THEOLOGICAL SEMINARY, NEW YORK

*Essay Index Reprint Series*

## BOOKS FOR LIBRARIES PRESS
### FREEPORT, NEW YORK

First Published 1930
Reprinted 1969

LIBRARY OF CONGRESS CATALOG CARD NUMBER:
69-17577

PRINTED IN THE UNITED STATES OF AMERICA

# PREFACE

Six of the essays in this book have already been published, and six now appear for the first time. Although at first sight they may seem to deal with a variety of unrelated topics, yet I am conscious of a unity underlying them all which has led me to gather them together into one volume. The source of this unity lies in the fourth and fifth essays, on Freedom, in which I have tried to indicate, as clearly as I can, what I am coming to think about some of the deepest and most central problems of philosophy. The other essays represent attempts to consider various questions of current interest from the point of view described in those two, and whatever claim my opinions may have to a hearing on such subjects as Birth Control, Sacraments, or the Reunion of Christendom, is due to their springing from roots in the central position arrived at through the discussion of Freedom.

Because the questions with which these two essays deal are deep and difficult, as well as central, the essays themselves may be found difficult—if not unintelligible—to readers unfamiliar with the technicalities of philosophy. I hope, however, that the remainder (with the possible exception of the last) will be readily intelligible to all who are interested in the present-day problems of Christianity, whether or no they be professional philosophers.

For myself, the publication of these essays marks a mid-way stage in the development of my thought. I am becoming aware of growing into a more and more consistent and thoroughgoing philosophical position, which some day I hope I may be able to try to exhibit as a systematic whole. But I must grow a lot more before my thought will be sufficiently mature for that, and meanwhile the essay form enables me to indicate the tendencies of the growth in various directions, while allowing me to leave unfilled the gaps which I am not yet ready to fill. It is my hope that by publishing at this stage I may receive, through the kindness of my readers, such criticisms as may check my erring steps and set me straighter on the path of further development before it is too late.

Of the essays already published, the first appeared in the Report of the American Church Congress for 1926, published by The Macmillan Company of New York under the title of "The Church and Truth." The second, third, and most of the seventh have appeared in the *Hibbert Journal*, the sixth in the *Anglican Theological Review*, and the eighth in the *Interpreter*. I wish here to express my gratitude to the various editors and publishers for the permission which has been given me to reprint; and once again I want to express (though no words are adequate in which to do so) what I owe to my wife for her help to me while writing and in preparing the book for the press.

L. H.

R.M.S. *Carmania,*
  *September* 1929.

# CONTENTS

# ESSAYS IN
# CHRISTIAN PHILOSOPHY

## I.  PSYCHOLOGY AND RELIGIOUS BELIEF

ANYTHING that is to be said on this subject in the year of grace 1926 must of necessity be tentative.  The words " The New Psychology " in the programme of this year's Congress remind us how recent a thing is the present-day study of psychology.  Theologians and natural scientists are now at last beginning to develop a sense of perspective when they discuss the relations of their respective studies.  This was lacking in many of the discussions of the last century, and it is well-nigh impossible as yet to arrive at such a sense of perspective in the case of psychology.  For myself, I must confess that I cannot see through many of the problems presented by psychological inquiry, or estimate what contributions of permanent value that study will eventually prove to have made to our understanding of our faith. Moreover, the question is complicated by disagreements among psychologists.  When behaviourists are disputing with partisans of the unconscious, we must remember how dangerous is the temptation to become proportionately more dogmatic as we wander farther from our own fields of study. It is no rare thing for a psychologist or scientist who maintains an admirable caution in making statements about his own subject to plunge disastrously into the waters of philosophy or theology ; there are also, I regret to say, theologians who will maintain an equal caution on, let us say, the Christological problem, but will not hesitate to adjudicate between vitalism and mechanism, or between psychoanalysis and behaviourism.

Bearing in mind these cautions, let us approach our subject by glancing at the position of man upon earth. Man has behind him the age-long history of the evolutionary process. In this process, the principle of advance seems to be that the creature coming into a new environment develops the characteristics necessary for existence in that environment; it is a history of successive readjustments to new conditions.[1] When we survey the process as a whole we have to recognise two elements : absolute continuity throughout and yet the emergence of real differences of kind. It is a common error to over-emphasise one at the expense of the other, but just as there are real differences of colour between colours, although they can be arranged shading off into one another so that it is impossible to draw a line where one ends and the next begins, so we must not refuse to recognise real differences of kind at different stages of evolution because we cannot draw lines to mark the point at which the breaks come.

In the course of this continuous process there have come to exist beings whose characteristic quality is that as individuals they are self-conscious and are able to apprehend beauty, truth and goodness. We may not be able to draw a line to mark the point where the human exercise of intelligence ceased to be merely a biological function, the use of an instrument giving a certain advantage over rivals in the struggle for survival, and became the spiritual power of appreciating values for their own inherent worth. But despite the continuity of the process there is here a real difference of kind between the spiritual appreciation of values and the compassing of earthly ends. The high points of human achievement are to be found in the spiritual spheres of art, of learning and of conduct. It is in the works of a Shakespeare or a Beethoven, in the discoveries of a Galileo or the thoughts of an Immanuel Kant, in the lives of a George Washington or an Abraham Lincoln that the spirit of man attains its highest self-expression.

---

[1] Whether in making these adjustments the creature receives from the new environment the power to respond to it, or finds the opportunity to put forth powers already latent within, seems to me to be the point at issue in the discussion whether acquired characteristics are transmissible—one of those discussions which are not for the theologian to decide.

I cannot explain these highest achievements of mankind except on the hypothesis that they are fragmentary glimpses and graspings of a higher spiritual reality, revealed to us in every apprehension of truth, of beauty and of goodness. Man has behind him the heritage of the age-long process of physical evolution; his further advance is now to be not physical but spiritual. The environment to which he is to adjust himself is that spiritual reality of which he has fragmentary glimpses and apprehensions in art, in learning, and in conduct. In religion we go farther, and claim that this spiritual reality which inspires the artist, the thinker, and the seeker after righteousness is such that we can call it " Him," and enter into personal relations with Him.

Here, *mutatis mutandis*, we see reproduced at a higher stage what has been going on throughout the evolutionary process. We see a creature in touch with two environments, only in this case the one is the physical environment of his origin, the other the spiritual environment of his goal—God. As before, to make himself completely and comfortably adjusted to the original environment is the way of stagnation; the secret of advance is the strain and stress of adjustment to the new—new, that is, to the creature in the course of time, but existing from everlasting as the implicit goal of the whole process.

If this be so, when we examine the constitution of man, we shall expect to find as the most deeply rooted and primitive elements in him characteristics developed in the struggle to adjust himself to the earlier of his two environments. And these, it seems to me, are what are most prominent in the discoveries resulting from psychological investigation. The primitive instincts of self-preservation and of reproduction striving for expression along the lines of adjustment to a purely physical environment are the most deeply rooted things we know. But we shall also expect to find these instincts controlled in accordance with lives devoted to the pursuit of goodness, of truth, of beauty, of response to the love of God. And this, too, we find all around us. The pity is that sometimes the intensive study of psychology blinds men's eyes to this very obvious fact.

Being thus blinded, and looking on man as adequately

described when considered in relation to his original environment, some teachers attempt to show as a result of their psychological investigations that there is no ground for believing in the existence of that higher spiritual environment at all.  Such attempts may be illustrated by reference to two technical terms, rationalisation and projection. Rationalisation is the giving of a reason for believing or doing something which, as a matter of fact, we believe or do from some quite different motive.  Projection is the objectifying as an external reality of some imaginary entity.  Thus, combining the two, it may be held that a man for whom the buffetings of life are too great a burden to be borne finds relief and maintains the balance of his mind by " projecting " an imaginary omnipotent and beneficent companion.  This is the real origin of his belief in God (though he does not know it) ; the reasoned theological or philosophical arguments by which he defends it are really (though again he does not know it ; only psychology reveals it) rationalisations.

Now this argument is sometimes used in a wholesale manner as though it put out of court in advance all theological and philosophical arguments for belief in God.  But if so, it proves too much.  For think what it involves.  It assumes as the whole truth about man that he is a citizen of this world only, seeking a harmonious adjustment to the conditions of this world.  It is in his earthly needs that we are to find the true motive of his beliefs and practices.  Why, then, should we make an exception of the belief of the psychologist who is thus expounding his views to us ? Suppose we retort that his explanation of our belief in God is itself a rationalisation of his egoistic instinct which demands expression (though he does not know it) along the lines of demonstrating his superiority to ourselves.  He will almost certainly repudiate the suggestion, and maintain that he is only telling us the truth.  It is only a disinterested love of truth which has led him to disturb our cherished beliefs.

There is, then, truth to be discovered, and there is the possibility of disinterested love of truth in the life of man. But grant this, and how can you explain it except as a glimpse of that higher environment we are striving to reach ?  There *are*, then, arguments which are not rationalisations, and our arguments for belief in God must be examined on their own merits, not put out of court unheard.

Indeed, there would be no point in discovering the existence of rationalisation and projection among the activities of the human mind, unless this were done with a view to discovering which among our beliefs are in truth to be condemned on this ground and which are not. I said at the beginning that it is difficult as yet to determine how much of permanent value the study of psychology will eventually prove to have contributed to our understanding of our faith, and that I cannot at present see my way through all the problems it presents. Among these problems, one is that of the extent to which certain states of mind sometimes found in certain religious people are to be regarded as rationalisations, or their beliefs as projections. For both rationalisations and projections do undoubtedly exist. Our task is to detect and dispel them.[1]

But I am not convinced that in order to detect and dispel them we must always substitute for the method of rational argument that of psychological investigation. Otherwise, as I said above, in order to weigh the value of a psychological argument we should not have to consider the argument but to psychoanalyse the psychologist. Moreover, there is still room for such arguments as those by which philosophers argue for the reasonableness of interpreting reality in terms of personality, and still mankind has to face the fact of Jesus Christ in the pages of history and to try to find a place for Him in the order of the universe.

To sum up. It seems to me that, apart from religion, the highest achievements of the spirit of man are found in the fields of art, of learning and of conduct. These achievements imply that man cannot be accounted for merely as constructed to find perfect adjustment to the sphere in which he arises ; he can only be true to the law of his past evolutionary heritage if he is striving onwards and upwards to adjust himself to a higher spiritual environment revealed to him in those fields. His past heritage explains the deep-rooted primitive instincts discovered in him by the psychologist,

---

[1] Similarly, we need to investigate to what extent human activities can be accounted for on behaviourist lines.

but that discovery must not blind us to the fact that he is also in touch with the higher environment—a fact implicit in the existence of the psychologist himself with his disinterested love of truth. It is in the truth that he has put his trust, and because he has put his trust in it he hopes not to be put to confusion; the truth is his stronghold whereunto he always resorts; it is the thing that he longs for, his hope even from his youth; he hopes that it may continue to possess him in his old age when he is grey-headed, that he may show its strength to his own generation and its power to all them that are yet for to come. May we not hope that either in this world or the next, he may have his eyes opened and come to see that (though he knew it not) the true interpretation of his own devotion to truth is the Psalmist's language of personal devotion to God?

## II. THE SELF AND "THE UNCONSCIOUS"

THE early Christians and their contemporaries lived, so they thought, among a large population of unseen spirits, powerful for good or evil. A kind of natural pessimism seems to have led most of those who paid much attention to the existence of this unseen population to have chiefly in mind those spirits which were evil. By an inference hardly surprising under the circumstances, they ascribed various ills in human life, especially ills which befell the mind, to the agency of these malignant powers. Men were said to be under the influence of, or to be possessed by, devils. But these ills were not incapable of cure. One might meet a healer who had power in the spirit world and was stronger than the devils, who would drive them away or cast them out, and so free the victims from their control. In the first few centuries of our era there were many who were thought so to have been cured.

We live to-day, so we think, with our minds shading off into a vast region called " the unconscious," the home of various " complexes," powerful for good or evil in our lives. When we think much of these, a kind of pessimism is apt to seize us, and our imagination is prone to become captive to the fear lest some evil complex which now, perhaps, lies hidden in " our unconscious " may some day rise up with evil portent for our future. It is not surprising that more and more we are coming to explain human action, and especially the action and mental condition of those who are deranged in mind, as due to the influence of these complexes. Moreover, with growing success we adopt this hypothesis in the treatment of mental diseases. Healers may be met who have power to bring to light the hidden complexes of " the unconscious," and, when the patient has seen them face to face, he is freed from their tyranny.  There are many men and women alive to-day who have so been cured.

We believe in complexes ; we do not believe in devils. What advantage has the one belief over the other ?  All the advantages, we should say, of being scientific instead of superstitious, of being based on the careful collection of instances and the verification of hypotheses in experience. So far so good, and I do not suppose that anyone who has taken the trouble to study any of the work of those experimentalists who have investigated the subject at first hand can doubt that great additions have been made to our knowledge worthy to be called assured results of science.  But truth is apt to be discovered entangled in much that is of less value, as precious metals are found embedded in base rock ; and to disentangle the assured results from less certain theories is a work always rendered necessary by any fresh advance in knowledge.  Here the layman may play his part by stating the problems which are suggested to his mind as he reflects on the work of the discoverer.  He is anxious to be scientific in his beliefs and not superstitious.  But sometimes he is puzzled as to how much in what is offered him is strictly scientific, and, if he wishes for truth, he must put his questions.

Devils, he gathers, are not scientific.  At any rate it is not usually claimed on their behalf that they are.  " The unconscious," on the other hand, does claim to be a scientific discovery, and to a large extent it makes good its claim. Men probe into its depths, and find what their previous experience would lead them to expect.  But frequently it is not merely " the unconscious " of which we hear ; it is " the unconscious self " of which men speak.  The complexes which may influence Jones's life are found in Jones's " unconscious self."  It is here that the puzzle begins.

Let us take our stand alongside the early Christian.  We are confronted with Jones whose mind is out of order. It seems simple to say that the facts are the same for us both, only we explain them differently.  The early Christian says " devils."  We say " complexes."  But the difference between us is deeper than at first sight appears.  The early Christian has little doubt about what he means by " Jones."

Jones is a man such as he is himself, with a clearly defined body, soul and spirit, who has got his mind into the power of devils. But for us Jones is a self of which only a small part is known either to us or to him. It is nothing clearly defined. Like an iceberg floating in the sea with vast masses hidden from view, Jones has vast depths in his self " beneath the threshold of consciousness "—his consciousness and ours.

Here at once, when we speak of Jones's " unconscious self," there is an ambiguity in the word " unconscious." It means, of course, that there is more in Jones than he knows of. But does it also mean that Jones is capable of thinking without knowing it ? Is it merely as an object of thought that he exists below as well as above the threshold of consciousness, or is he to be found there as thinking subject too ? It is clear from the language used that both are often included. We are shown facts which are said to be explicable only on the theory of so-called " unconscious cerebration." The " unconscious self " is an active mental entity.

This is a very difficult conception indeed. Thought is known to us in the activity of thinking, as will in the activity of willing, and emotion in the activity of feeling ; while what we mean by " the self " is the subject of these activities. When Descartes tried to find something of whose existence he could be absolutely sure, he found it in himself as the subject of consciousness—*cogito ergo sum*. But now it is the self as unconscious of its own activities that we are interested in—a curiously objectivist result of that devotion to psychology initiated by the subjectivism of Descartes.

It is probable that the language of John Locke is largely responsible for this turn of events. His famous description of the mind as a *tabula rasa* is clearly capable of interpretation in such a way as to open the door for the present development. It may suggest that the mind is not an active subject of consciousness, but a passive some*thing* on which impressions make their mark. It is fatally easy to forget that the analogy of the clean sheet of paper is only an analogy, to forget the element of consciousness in the mind under the influence of the metaphor. If we approach the subject thinking of the mind as receiving impressions in the same way as the sheet of paper receives the impressions of a pencil, it is easy to transfer to the mind the unconsciousness of the paper. But in doing this, disguise it as we will, there is a materialism in our thought. We are thinking of the mind, not as the spiritually alive subject of consciousness, but as some sort of a substance existing whether conscious or no. We may not, perhaps, think of it as extended in space, but we certainly think of it as extended in time; and what do we mean by " matter " if it be not that which is unconscious and extended ? The idea of the mind, or of the self, as some sort of an unconscious substance is undoubtedly materialistic. The layman, then, cannot but ask if he can only accept what is scientific at the cost of becoming a materialist.

The question is, What is to be meant by the word " self " ? How is that word to be used ? Is it to be confined to the spiritually alive subject of consciousness, or must we make the plunge into materialism and speak of " the unconscious self " ? Are the facts of recent psychological discovery such as to drive us to this ? Or can we accept as " scientific " all that is being learned about " the unconscious " without going on to commit ourselves to belief in " unconscious selves " ? How much progress can we make towards assimilating the new knowledge while confining the use of the word " self " to the description of the subject of consciousness ?

So limiting our own use of the word, let us see how far we can get.

We will not at first consider " the unconscious " at all, but will ask what we mean by " the self " in the ordinary world of the plain man—the world of the early Christian. This is no easy question to answer, as any plain man may soon discover by reading such a book as Professor Laird's " Problems of the Self." But we may, perhaps, assume this much, that by a self we ordinarily mean a conscious subject of experiences with a certain continuity born of self-consciousness and memory. He is accustomed to distinguish himself from what in philosophy has been called the not-self, which we may perhaps call, in less pure but more ordinary English, his environment. We may not always be able to make up our minds where to draw the line between the self and the environment, but, if we have learned what Professor

Pringle-Pattison has to teach us, we shall not refuse to make distinctions because we cannot draw lines.

But if a self be a self-conscious unity of experiences, it is clear that we do not come into existence ready made, so to speak. The self is a growing being, and it grows by feeding upon the experiences provided for it by the environment. It learns *risu cognoscere matrem*, it hears nursery rhymes and is taught the alphabet, it reads books, plays games, looks at pictures, and listens to music. From this point of view, the world around—the world of the not-self which is its environment—exists to provide experiences which the self may weave, so to speak, into the fabric of itself. But it has a power of rejecting as well as of accepting the proffered experiences. My environment contains an infinity of potential experiences, among which only a certain number may go to the making of myself. Sometimes I can choose which I will experience. There are more books on my shelves than I am ever likely to be able to read : there are more unmarried women in the world than I can ever marry. Sometimes I cannot help undergoing an experience I would rather avoid. We need not now go further into this than to see that in the environment of the self are an infinite number of potential experiences of which it can actually experience only a certain number, and that it has some degree of choice over those which are to be woven into the fabric of its being.

We may, perhaps, express a doubt whether it is justifiable to include in a man's self, in the true sense, anything for which he cannot be held responsible. Certainly, the self in which a man is himself interested is that which, if he believes in a Day of Judgment, he expects then to be judged. He is, of course, directly responsible for certain elements in his environment as well as for his " self." If he has hung his room with lewd pictures, or has murdered a man and hidden his body in a wood, he has incurred very grave responsibilities. There is a relation of mutual interaction between the environment and the self. It can provide him with experiences, and he can wreak his will upon it. Moreover, since for each man the whole world of the not-self is his environment, it is different for each self, and, since for all practical purposes he only comes in touch with certain nearer ranges of it, in the case of each man we may speak of his particular environment. It is that which has influence upon him and provides those experiences which go to the making of himself. That, too, he in turn has influenced, and to some extent he is responsible for its condition.

Now, if the position thus briefly and inadequately sketched is a tenable one, is there any reason why the so-called " unconscious " should not be looked on as an extension of the environment rather than of the self?

First we must deal with the body. Is the physical body to be looked on as belonging to the self or to the environment? It seems to me necessary to assign it to the latter. It is, maybe, the nearest environment of the self; but it is environment for all its nearness, for it is material, and its work is to provide the self with experiences, not to experience them itself. But if we agree to class the body as environment, then at once a large element in " the unconscious " is already accounted for. Whatever of instincts, tendencies, passions, etc., we inherit by physical descent from our ancestors, come to us as materials to be woven into the fabric of ourselves or to be cast out and rejected; but only as accepted and woven in do they become part of the self. Perhaps when we become conscious of them we may refuse to admit them. Certainly, so long as they remain in " the unconscious " they are in our environment.

Then there are all those past experiences which we have forgotten, but which have left their mark upon us, as in the case of a woman who had been shut up in a dark cupboard at the mercy of the bogey man when she was a child, so that years afterwards she had an unreasoning fear of the dark which she could neither account for nor subdue until a healer " re-associated the complex " and set her free. Now in what would be a very common account of this case it is easy to see the pressing beyond its due of such an analogy as that of a wax tablet. We may think of a particle of ferrous matter falling on the surface of the wax and sinking in until the surface is again smooth, though the particle is now within, and of that particle being again drawn to the surface by a magnet. But what right have we to assume that the mind has an inside and an outside, a top and a bottom, an above the surface and a below the surface ?   These are all metaphors from space.   All that we are entitled to say is that a child had the experience of being shut up in the dark in great terror, and that from this she wove into the fabric of herself a fear of darkness and afterwards forgot how this fear had arisen—as she might have acquired the knowledge that two and two make four and afterwards forgotten where she first learned it.   Many years afterwards, in a state of trance, she recalls the incident.   But that incident, as a fact of past history, is an element in the environment of the mind at the present, which can be contemplated in memory just as the proceedings in Parliament to-day are an element in the environment and can be followed by sitting in the gallery or reading the newspapers.   The fact that things are sometimes remembered in a state of trance which are forgotten by the fully conscious mind is neither here nor there. The question is whether memory necessitates the belief that past events are *in* the mind as a particle of grit may be *in* a tray of wax.   If we do not hold the materialist conception of mind, which alone can justify us in refusing to recognise the purely metaphorical use of the word " in " as referred to the mind, we may surely conclude that to believe that past events are " in the unconscious mind " is mythology—like the belief in devils.

Then there are all those suppressed desires which may be revealed in our dreams.   Here again, it seems to me, the hypothesis of an " unconscious self " is unnecessary.   We have definitely refused to weave into the fabric of ourselves some possible and offered experience.   What if we do remember that offer again at a time when the reins of our self-control are slackened by sleep ?   It is no more part of our selves now than it was then.

It would be impossible in a brief essay such as this to attempt to deal with the whole catalogue of such contents of " the unconscious " as have been discovered.   That, moreover, were a task better attempted by someone more familiar with them than that inquiring layman, the present writer. All he can do is to suggest a possible hypothesis for some competent student to verify.

The hypothesis, in brief, is this.   In our ordinary waking life we are in touch with an environment which provides us with experiences, and we grow by weaving them into the fabric of our selves. The investigation of consciousness in other states than that of waking life seems to reveal the fact that this environment is not all that can go to the making of us—we are also in touch with " the unconscious." I would suggest that what we mean by " the unconscious " is a vast extension of the range of our possible experiences, of the environment of our selves. What each of us can there come in touch with will vary in each case, as in the environment of our waking life. Each has " his environment " in the one sphere as in the other, and there are elements in both for which he is responsible. What are the contents of that environment which we call " the unconscious " only patient investigation can reveal. There would seem at any rate to be the forgotten facts of our past history—but are there only our own past experiences ? Who can say ? Perhaps one day we may even discover devils, if not God Himself.

Sometimes I wonder, do the devils laugh ?

## III.  SIN AND ITS REMEDY IN THE LIGHT
## OF PSYCHOLOGY

### I

IN ordinary Christian teaching the matter of sin and its
remedy is commonly stated somewhat as follows : Sin is
defined as conscious disobedience to God's will, a definition
which implies belief in a God whose will is discoverable, and
in the possession by man of freedom to obey or disobey it.
When the sin has been committed, it leaves the sinner in a
position in which by himself he cannot undo or make good
the evil that has been done.   This deadlock is met by the
doctrine of the Atonement regarded as an act of God making
possible the neutralising of the evil effects of sin, both those
which linger on in the state of the sinner's soul and those which
remain elsewhere—" God in Christ reconciling the world unto
Himself." [1]   What is required of the sinner in order that he
may benefit by this act of God is repentance—that is to say,
sorrow for his sin, confession of his sin, and purpose of
amendment.   When he repents, God sees to the rest.   This is
the fundamental message of Christianity, that as a result of
the act of God in Christ sins repented are sins forgiven, and
the message is one and the same whether it be declared by
preacher from the pulpit or by priest from altar steps or
confessional chair.

It is important to notice that the practice which arises out
of this teaching depends on faith in the truth of the doctrine
taught, on faith in the reality of God and the moral order.
The practice is not primarily a psychological device, but an
attempt to train human life in accordance with a belief as to
the nature of reality.   Where this belief is lacking, the practice

[1] 2 Cor. v. 19.

will be lacking too, and some other diagnosis must be made of the trouble which we have been accustomed to regard as a "state of sin." Here is a subject on the border line of the territory where philosophy and psychology overlap; and a philosophical theologian may be pardoned for looking across the boundary into the fields of his brother students, the psychologists, to see what light on his own problems may be gathered from their researches.

There would seem to be two main schools of thought among recent students of psychology which for convenience may be called the psychoanalytic and the behaviourist. By "psychoanalytic" I do not mean exclusively "Freudian," but any psychology in which "psychic" events are recognised as distinct from physical. By "behaviourist" I mean that school of thought which hopes to account for all events, including human actions, by the formula "stimulus-reflex," allowing no initiating power to conscious human intention. This point of view is perhaps best described by reference to the now famous experiments of Pavlov on canine salivation. It was found that a dog's mouth waters at the approach of appetising food, and that other stimuli, by being at first combined with the food and then substituted for it, could be made to produce the same effect. This effect was involuntary on the part of the dog, a purely physical reflex action.

In attempting to understand how it is that psychology has come to take this twofold course, I would suggest the following explanation. In our ordinary, everyday outlook, before we begin to philosophise or psychologise (if one may coin the word) we commonly distinguish between events which we ascribe to the physical order and events which we ascribe to conscious purpose. The former we think of as proceeding in accordance with a sequence of cause and effect which we commonly call "mechanistic," the latter as free acts of will. In human life we should have no hesitation in placing the processes of respiration and digestion in the former class, and distinguishing them from acts of which we might say, "I made up my mind to do that." But while in clear instances of each we seem to be able to distinguish these two classes of events, there is an obscure area on the border line between the two in which it is difficult to say to which class a particular event should be referred. Take, for example, that stage in the growth of a boy when he becomes aware of the attractions of the other sex. He has been accustomed to run about with other boys, and possibly to regard girls—and boys who show a liking for the society of girls—as " silly." But now his habits of life change. If a pretty girl comes into the room or the railway carriage where he is, he " ͟its up and takes notice." What is happening ?

The psychoanalyst and the behaviourist seem to differ by taking as their guiding principle of interpretation one or other of those classes of events which in some instances are clearly distinguishable. They set out, as it were, from opposite shores to explore the uncharted sea between the two. To the behaviourist, what is happening in the boy is a physico-chemical reaction, comparable to the canine salivation in the presence of food. But to the psychoanalyst, what is happening is a purposive striving after some desired satisfaction. Only, as the boy cannot be accused of consciously either desiring the satisfaction or striving after it, some subject of the desire and of the purposive activity has to be found, and he finds himself driven to the mythology of " the unconscious self." Another illustration of the same cleavage of thought, taken from life at the sub-human level, is provided by the question Why does a hen sit on her eggs ? " Maternal instinct, aiming at the propagation of the species," says one school. " Nonsense," says the other ; " it is because a local inflammation on the under side of the hen is soothed by contact with the smooth warm surface of the eggs. Irritate a capon with red pepper, and it will sit just as well as any hen. It is nothing but reaction to stimulus, just like the dog's reaction to the scent of food."

But the fact remains that the result of this correspondence between maternal inflammation and the soothing power of the eggs does issue in the chickens. It looks as though each school of thought had got hold of one side of the truth ; as though what the facts reveal is an order of events which, regarded from the outside, bear all the marks of being both mechanistic and purposive, but cannot be ascribed to any particular purposer. The hen's action does fulfil the purpose of race preservation, but the hen is innocent of aiming at any such thing. The boy is seeking a satisfaction the fulfilment of which will contribute to the life of the human race, but he may be quite unaware of the fact.

To meet this situation some psychologists are inclined to suggest the hypothesis of some kind of vital urge which animates creation. Whether they call it urge, or *élan vital*, or *libido*, or what not, makes little difference. Whether it be described in English, French, or Latin, it is an attempt to describe that element in the phenomena of life which goes beyond mere machinery but is not the conscious purposive activity of the individual concerned. But this hypothesis is surely insufficient. It is a timid, half-hearted approach towards a solution of the problem. It leaves out just the crucial element required, that of intelligent purposiveness. It is more than a universal urge that is required to explain the facts : it is a universal purpose. In many cases the formula which seems most adequate is one which speaks of a mechanism serving the universal purposiveness. But to speak of the " universal purpose " is to speak of God. Purposes without any purposer are nonsense, and though we may acquit the boy and the hen of being the purposers, we cannot recognise the action as purposive without sooner or later being driven either to mythology or to God. Though either school in psychology, when standing alone, may dispense with God (along with a number of other awkward facts to which a blind eye has to be turned), if one tries to allow for what is true in both schools, one needs the hypothesis of God to make the complementary truths hang together.

## II

It would seem that in many cases, so far as the interpretation of the immediate facts is concerned, the account given by the behaviourist is to be preferred to that of the psychoanalyst, and that we owe a debt of gratitude to the behaviourist school for recalling us to sanity from some of the wilder speculations of their opponents. This conclusion is confirmed when we look back over the past history of man, both human and pre-human. In the history of human development it seems to be true that the physical organism comes first in time, and functions as a " going concern " before there supervenes upon it that potentiality of self-conscious experience which we call the self or soul. Throughout the history of the previous development of the physical organism the principle of progress seems to be that of adjustment or adaptation to fresh environment. Where there is perfect adjustment to the *status quo* there is stagnation. Progress is born of the struggle to live in unprecedented circumstances. But the creatures in this struggle must not be personified, as though they were consciously striving after this end. Their adaptation may be described on behaviourist lines, as reflex reactions to fresh stimuli.

When in this way the physical creature has reached a certain state of complex, differentiated organisation of structure, there appears that self-conscious subject of its experiences which we call man. To use crudely metaphorical language, one may perhaps think of this self-conscious purposive life as being at first like a faint and flickering wisp of flame on the surface of that " going concern," the body. The whole point of life on earth is that this flickering flame, this potentiality of self-conscious purposive life, this embryo self or soul, shall grow into full selfhood or soulhood by extending its control over that " going concern," and taking up its behaviouristic functioning into its own purposive self-determination. The experiences mediated through each particular body go to the making of each self or soul what it is ; it grows and develops as the subject of these experiences, apart from which it has no being at all. They give it its concrete character and its distinct characteristics. But if it is to grow, it must assert its mastery over that from which it draws its content. How is this to be ?

If in looking over the course of *human* history we ask what are the high points of human achievement, we find them preeminently in the fields of art, learning and conduct. In other words, when the stage of physical development has been reached at which man exists as a self-conscious, purposive subject of bodily experiences, the direction in which further progress can take place is in the spiritual sphere. It is hard to account for man's progress in art, learning and conduct except as springing from his glimpses of the eternal beauty, truth and goodness, from graspings at that higher spiritual environment to which he is trying to adjust himself. In religion we claim to hold personal converse with Him who is the source of those glimpses of the eternal which have inspired the artist, the thinker and the man of noble life.

But still, as before, struggle to readjust is the secret of progress ; only now the struggle is that of an individual capable of knowing what he is doing and of consciously choosing either to make the effort or to refuse to do so. He exists as the subject of the experiences of a body fashioned by centuries of adaptation to adjust itself to the physical environment of this world. Its natural tendency is to react harmoniously to the *status quo*. But the man has had his glimpse of the world beyond, and if, like St. Paul, he is to be able to say " Wherefore I was not disobedient unto the heavenly vision," [1] he must face the struggle of adjusting himself to the society of God. *What he is made of* is provided by the experiences which come to him through the body ; *what sort of a soul he makes of himself* depends on the way in which he controls these experiences. Shall it be in an effort to climb the steep ascent of heaven, or to settle down in comfortable adaptation to the world in which he starts ?   " My son, if thou come to serve the Lord, prepare thy soul for temptation." [2]

## III

The recognition of this tension or struggle as the law of progress in life is of the first importance in considering the practical question of meeting temptation. It is commonly supposed that there are two ways of meeting temptation : either to withstand it or to give way to it. But to leave the matter there is to neglect a distinction that is vital from the psychological standpoint. There are two ways of resisting. A man may resist, relying on his own natural strength, from such motives as aspiration after high ideals, or self-respect, or pride, or fear of social disapproval. But he may also resist in humble reliance on the grace of God, knowing full well that if left to himself he would be the first to give way. So the

[1] Acts xxvi. 19.                         [2] Ecclus. ii. 1.

ways of meeting temptation open to a man are not two but three :

(a) Give way.

(b) Resist in reliance on himself.

(c) Resist in humble self-distrust and reliance on God.

I venture to assert that it is in the middle course that there lies the great danger of psychopathic trouble. It is one of the most curious facts that many psychologists, to judge from their writings, seem to regard the typically religious man as belonging to this class, as likely to be shocked and indignant when told that at heart he is unclean. It makes one wonder what kind of religion can be practised in the spheres where psychologists forgather, for surely the first lesson in practical Christianity is to learn to say humbly and sincerely, " I know that left to myself I am by nature sinful, and only by the grace of God in Christ can I be saved from myself."

It is one of the great contributions to practical therapeutics made by the psychoanalytical school to have shown that many psychopathic ills are due to a concealed struggle with some temptation hidden out of sight in the sick man's life. The psychoanalyst drags up the fact of this struggle into the light of day, and makes the man look at it. What is the next step to be ? I very much fear that, for want of any practical acquaintance with the third way of meeting temptation mentioned above, some psychoanalysts are driven to recommend the first. Would that all were like one leading practitioner who, after revealing to a patient that his trouble was due to a sexual conflict which he would not face, then said to him : " It is not my duty to be your moral adviser, but I say this to you as your doctor. You now know the cause of your trouble. You can either continue the struggle or seek to solve it by indulging your desire. The former course is no more dangerous than the latter. It was the concealment, the repression, the refusal to face the issue, that caused the trouble. A fight in the open, so long as it is kept in the open, is nothing to be afraid of."

But a fight in the open, when waged by a man in reliance on his own strength, is apt to be a losing battle, and to lead to the repression which is dangerous. The way to a full, rich and free life is neither by scaling down our moral principles to suit our bodily desires, nor by trusting in our own strength to stem the reactionary trend of the body's inherited habits.  It is by recognising that as this struggle is the very material out of which progress is wrought, and as by ourselves we are not equal to it, we will listen to the voice of Christ, and try to verify in our own experience what was discovered by St. Paul. " He that abideth in me, and I in him, the same bringeth forth much fruit : for without me ye can do nothing." [1]  " I can do all things through Christ which strengtheneth me." [2]

## IV

When now at last we turn to consider directly the subject of sin and its remedy, we shall do well to remember the general principle of all psychological treatment, whether preventive or curative.  This may be described as education to face reality.  The psychopathic trouble is caused by failure to progress in this education, by refusal to meet the ever-developing claims made by reality upon the growing man or woman, by turning aside to take refuge in fixation or phantasy or both.

If this be so, the question of the treatment required in any particular case will clearly depend on the nature of reality, and the nature of the particular failure to comply with its demands.  Now, if reality include such factors as

(1) God, against whom we can and do sin;

(2) Our inability to avoid this without His help;

(3) Our inability to make good the evil done when we do sin;

(4) The adequacy of God's act of atonement to do this

—then the governing principle of psychological treatment demands that the soul be brought to face the fact of these important elements in reality and to adjust himself or herself to them.  This is what is done in confession and absolution. Whether or no reality is such as is presupposed by this practice is not itself primarily a psychological but a philosophical question.  But, given the philosophical conviction that it is so, then the traditional practice based upon this conviction would seem to be based on sound psychological principles.

[1] Jn. xv. 5.                    [2] Phil. iv. 13.

But here a word of caution is necessary.

Because we recognise in sin unrepented and unforgiven a genuine cause of psychopathic trouble, we must not be carried away to regard it as the only such cause. It is surely one among many, and what is most greatly needed in the treatment of any case is careful diagnosis and delimitation of area. By way of rough guidance we may classify cases into three :

(a) Cases with no moral implications, e.g. an obsessive fear of dark places caused by having been shut up in a black cupboard when a child.

(b) Cases with clear moral and no psychopathic implications, e.g. the majority of confessions of normal persons.

(c) Cases intermediate between these, in which it may be most difficult to decide just what the nature of the trouble is.

What is required is surely co-operation between those who approach the subject from the religious and the psycho-therapeutic standpoints. The priest must always be ready to acknowledge the possibility that in a particular case what at first sight looked like sin may be more of the nature of disease, and to recommend his patient for psychotherapeutic treatment. Conversely, the psychiatrist, when convinced that an element of moral responsibility for the trouble is present, must avoid driving the trouble deeper in by allowing the patient to ignore that responsibility and its need of treatment through penitence and absolution.

The question is that of the kind of adjustment needed in particular cases. Psychological research may have complicated the problem of diagnosis, but where the readjustment required is that between a sinner and the God against whom he has sinned, faith in the sacrifice of Calvary, issuing in confession and the grateful acceptance of the gift of absolution, appears to be psychologically, as well as theologically, the only sound remedy.

# IV. THE QUESTION OF FREEDOM

## I

ONE of the many stories current in Oxford concerning Benjamin Jowett tells of an occasion when an undergraduate read him a lengthy essay conclusively disproving the existence of freedom of the will. The Master listened patiently to the end, and then made one comment : " That's great nonsense. There's all the difference in the world between your going out of this room by yourself and my kicking you out." Such a rough-and-ready disposition of one of the most perplexing problems of philosophy may have been a salutary dose of medicine for a sophisticated undergraduate, but it is hardly likely to satisfy a serious inquirer any more than Dr. Johnson's claim to refute Berkeley by kicking a stone. It is of value, nevertheless, as clearly describing a distinction which we all make in everyday life, when we are not philosophising. We do distinguish between going out of a room " of our own will " (as we say) and being pushed out by some external force, such as a fellow-man's hand and boot, or a gas explosion, and we commonly think of the former act as being free in contrast with the latter which is enforced.

Like so many things which in our everyday life we take for granted as " simple facts," this distinction turns out, when investigated, to be far from simple, and the account of the controversies between those who have maintained and those who have denied its validity, and of the efforts made among the former party to decide which events belong to which class, occupy no small portion of the history of philosophy. The importance of the question for the study of Christian philosophy needs no emphasis. Christian thought has had to wrestle with it from time to time as it has come to the fore again and again. In these days the study of psychology has

given it a new significance.    In many universities it is tacitly
assumed in the department of psychology that belief in human
freedom, as assumed in Dr. Jowett's distinction, is an outworn
relic of a pre-scientific age, and it is in the light of current
psychological study that the question of freedom must be
considered to-day.

In the essay on " Sin and its Remedy " I have already in-
dicated the general lines on which I shall approach the problem
of Freedom, and have attempted to arrive at some estimate of
the kind of help which may be expected from psychological
study.    In what follows I shall take for granted the argument
of that essay, attempting to strengthen some of its foundations
and to develop some of its implications as they bear on the
question before us.    Now, as before, I shall start with our
everyday distinction between events which we assign to a
" mechanistic " sequence of cause and effect, and events
which we describe by saying " I made up my mind to do that " ;
and will try to examine rather more closely than before certain
aspects of the problem provided by this distinction.    But
now we can take for granted in its general outline the conception of the self which makes up its mind as a being whose
content is given by and through the pre-existing bodily
" machine," and whose history on earth is the history of
its gradual growth in individual self-consciousness and self-
control.

As among psychologists it is the behaviourist who most
directly challenges any such conception of the self, he must
have our first attention.    But before offering some criticisms
of his position it will be well to remind ourselves that we have
no more desire than has the behaviourist, or any other kind of
determinist, to argue for the existence of any ultimate " chanciness " in events.    We do not wish to find a place for chance,
but to criticise the assumption that chance is the only alternative to mechanistic sequence.    For us, as for those from whom
we differ, the universe is a coherent whole, and there is no
room in it for ultimately unrelated and inexplicable events,
which remain, as it were, " surds " in the system.    The
question is that of the nature of the whole system, whether
it is adequately conceived as mechanistic, or whether it is
better interpreted in the light of willed events, and what

status within it is to be given to the events which make up the life of a human being.

The inquirer who is conducting an investigation in the world of mechanistic sequence takes that world for granted, and attempts to discover particular connections which obtain within it. Thus a doctor seeks for the cause of cancer. He is not seeking to answer the question " How does natural causation work in general ? "—he takes that for granted and asks, " Given the system of natural causation, what events in that system are connected with this cancerous growth in the human body ? " Similarly, we do not profess to be able to give any *general* account of why or how human beings act as they do, beyond saying that they act as a result of making up their minds to do so. The grounds on which this or that particular act was done can be explained, but only by taking for granted the existence of the world of willed or purposive events. This purposive order, or world of willed events, is, as a matter of fact, at least as well known to us as the order of natural causation ; we imply its existence whenever we ask such a question as " Why on earth did you do that ? "—a question which invites a man to explain his act to us as to people who know what it is to make up their minds to act on reasonable grounds.

There would seem to be this *prima facie* difference between the two orders, that in the case of an event in the mechanistic system its explanation has to be sought in the previously existent conditions, while a purposive event is explained by reference to the future, to what it was aiming at. Attempts have been made to get round this on the ground that the goal must be grasped in consciousness and desired before the act can be done, so that the goal-grasped-and-willed can be regarded as the mechanistic cause of the resulting act. Granted the assumption that mechanistic causation is the only possible explanation of any and every event, this might be satisfactory ; but unfortunately the assumption that has to be taken for granted is the conclusion that had to be proved. Take this away, and all that has been said is that an act of will has to be willed before it can be executed, and this proves nothing. One is equally justified, at this preliminary stage, in assuming that an act of will is an event *sui generis*, inexplicable in terms of mechanistic causation ; and to claim the relief that comes from being under no necessity to adapt the forward-looking purposiveness of human life to the Procrustean bed of determination *a tergo*. The further examination of these two assumptions is to form the subject of the rest of this essay.

## II

We start, then, from our everyday distinction between mechanistic and willed events. It is the contention of the behaviourist that this distinction is a false one, and that the latter events turn out on examination to be instances of the former in disguise. But this contention raises at least four difficulties, which may be stated as follows :

1. At the very outset one's breath is taken away by the boundless optimism of the hypothesis. What is asserted is not merely that *some* events which we thought to owe their existence to their being willed do not really do so, but that there are no truly willed events at all. As an example of what is implied let us consider what happens in the tossing of a coin. When the initial impetus has been given which sends the penny spinning in the air, its movements proceed according to determinate mechanistic sequence, and whether it ultimately comes down heads or tails is only unpredictable by us because we have no instruments of adequate complexity and refinement to make the necessary observations and calculations. But suppose we discover that the coin has been loaded so as to ensure its falling with a certain side up. We should naturally think that factors of another order had entered into the situation, factors which are not patient of the same kind of measurement and calculation as those which govern the behaviour of the coin after it has left the spinner's hand.[1] It is this which the behaviourist denies,

---

[1] Let it be said once again that it is not a question of chance or no chance. There is no more chance in the loading of the coin than in the behaviour of the spun coin. Indeed, there is less, and it may be suggested that the only real chance we ever experience is deliberately willed chance. In the above instance such element of chance as there is is due to the coin being deliberately spun in such a way as to outstrip our capacity for predicting its fall. Chance is due to willed concealment of the factors necessary for apprehension, and only exists in a world of beings who conduct their lives to some extent on a basis of will. The experience of such chance is the origin of our illusory ascription of chance to events in the mechanistic world. Cp. below, p. 40.

optimistically heralding the advent of the day when the surreptitious doctoring of the penny will be clearly exhibited as a process of precisely the same order as its career from thumb-nail to ground. No doubt he has some scores to his credit; no doubt he has revealed to us that some events, which appeared at first sight to be willed, were not—just as psychoanalysts have revealed to us that some beliefs which we thought to be genuine convictions were in truth " projections " or " rationalisations." But as in the one case, so in the other, we may justifiably pause before jumping to the conclusion that evidence which is of use to enable us to distinguish false from true claimants to the status of conviction or action is fatal to the existence of any true claimants at all.

2. It is not sufficient, of course, to call attention to the behaviourist's optimism in order to refute his position. By this time we Christians should have learned through sad experience the folly of any Spencerian tendency to build our faith on the gaps in scientific discovery simply because they are gaps. We must have some more positive ground for doubting that an event is patient of mechanistic interpretation than the fact that the way to such an interpretation has not as yet been found. Are there any reasonable grounds for thinking that in his optimism the behaviourist is unreasonably optimistic?

We may here take up again a point previously mentioned, and call attention to the fact that, at starting, the willed order has at least as good a claim to our respect as the mechanistic. In refusing to accede to the request that we should regard the loading of the coin as parallel to its subsequent movements in the air, we are not making an obscurantist refusal to abandon the unknown for the known. *We know very well what it means to cheat*—better, indeed, than what it means to be sent spinning through the air. Even when we do experience the latter sensation, it remains inexplicable brute fact to us until interpreted in terms of will; a football game is easier to understand than a railway accident, and the universe does not become more explicable if collisions on the football field are regarded as obscurer examples of what happens when a crowd of people is hit by a tornado. Our first ground for not accepting the behaviourist optimism is that we feel there is need for caution before abandoning what we seem to understand for what is quite opaque to us, on the strength of evidence which covers so little of the required ground.

It has been often observed that a thing may be so well known to us that we take it for granted and fail to observe its existence. This seems to have happened once again in the case of the behaviourists' attitude to will. Their exposition of human nature is combined with reproaches levelled against those who do not accept it, who are accused of shutting their eyes to the truth and standing in the way of a remoulding of human society nearer the heart's desire. Now there is no doubt that for such applied sciences as that of advertising behaviourism *does work*—up to certain limits often overlooked—and there is no doubt of its efficiency as an instrument of social control.[1] Hypnotised by evidence of success in regimenting human beings, the behaviourist is blind to the fact that someone must do the regimenting and must presumably have some idea of the direction in which he wishes it to proceed. If the awkward question is raised, the answer is postponed on the ground that there has not yet been time for sufficient behaviourist practice on which to work out the behaviourist ethics of the future, in which everything will be satisfactorily explained. In the meantime, the ideal aimed at seems to be to get rid of all unnecessary accompaniments to efficient functioning as breadearners. God for the behaviourist (had he any use for the conception) would be " the economic-man " writ large, and it is hardly surprising that Dr. J. B. Watson, the high-priest of the cult, confesses himself unable to give any rational grounds for wanting to live. In this he is quite consistent : if there be nothing but blind mechanistic determination there are no rational grounds for anything ; and if there are no rational grounds for anything it is useless to ask the behaviourist why he writes books apparently aimed at inducing his reader on rational grounds to change his opinions. But those of us who still retain our faith in reason cannot but prefer the rationality of his assumptions to the irrationality of his conclusions, and claim his actions as evidence that he

[1] But see below, p. 42.

knows how to make use of his will even while pretending that no intelligible meaning can be attached to the idea of it.

3. We thus approach a more fundamental criticism of the whole behaviouristic scheme, finding it wanting because content to rest in an unintelligible mechanism which simply has to be accepted, as Professor Alexander would say, " with natural piety." Intellectually we are to bow our heads before an ultimate mystery which is unworthy of our worship. In this the behaviourist is intellectually (as he is also morally) reactionary; his philosophy is akin to that of Thales and Anaximander (whose importance in the history of thought is that they prepared the way for Anaxagoras), and if he had any religion it would belong to the pre-prophetic era when the will of God was to be sought through dreams, or the casting of lots, or wizards that peeped and muttered. Since those days philosophy, religion and science have all made some progress, and the method which has been found fertile in each of those fields has been that of a rational self-criticism based on the postulate of the fundamental intelligibility of reality to man's rational consciousness. Those of us who are theologians are sufficiently familiar with obscurantism masquerading as latter-day wisdom to be able to recognise the breed in our excursions abroad into the realms of psychology.

It is the insistent pressure of the demand for intelligibility which underlies the development of all idealist philosophy; but it is essential to any sane idealism to emphasise the point that the pressure that drives the mind onwards is all of a piece throughout. The same spirit which forbids a man to rest content with a single brute fact as " given," and drives him on to seek to understand it in relation to its environment— this spirit, which thus creates a scientist, creates also a philosopher when it forbids a man to rest content with the systematised order of events as discovered by the sciences, and drives him on to seek a meaning in it. The unity of the spirit has at times tended to become obscured, owing to the intense degree of specialisation demanded of modern students by the vast and complex mass of information which has been acquired through scientific research. Hence comes a blindness which issues on the one side in insanely idealistic

philosophy, and on the other in obscurantist science. Insane idealism is that which thinks itself free to ignore the
contributions of the sciences as describing the reality which
it is trying to understand, while obscurantist science is well
illustrated by the remark of a biologist of my acquaintance
who, after listening to Mr. H. W. B. Joseph's Herbert Spencer
Lecture on "The Concept of Evolution," [1] dismissed it
with the remark "Of course that is a philosopher's argument,
not a scientist's." Among other products of the war
between insane idealism and obscurantist science are the
misguided pacifists on either side—scientists who take refuge
in irrational religions on the ground that their scientific
research has nothing to do with God's self-revelation, and
philosophers who glory in having abandoned the task to
which they were called.

Happily there are signs here (as elsewhere) of a growing
dissatisfaction with war; a growing appreciation of that
unity of the spirit which must be the bond of peace between
scientist and philosopher. We may call in evidence the
insight with which that gallant upholder of sane idealism, the
late Bernard Bosanquet, rejected all accounts of the physical
world which involved treating it as essentially different from
that which the sciences find it to be,[2] and regarded as central
in his thought the conviction that while the world of scientific
observation demands to be seen in the light of a larger whole
in order to be intelligible, it is by this process not destroyed
but established. On the other side, there is the witness of
such facts as Professor Whitehead summarises in his "Science
and the Modern World," [3] where he shows how in the
historical development of scientific research the spirit of the
inquiry, having conceived it in the womb of rationalism and
given it birth, is now driving it on willy-nilly into philosophy
by the irresistible logic of its own pursuit of understanding.

If this be true, then the behaviourist contentment with
an unintelligible mechanistic order as ultimate is reactionary,
not only from the point of view of philosophy but also from

---

[1] Oxford University Press, 1924. This contains in a brief compass the
best criticism known to me of the presuppositions on which the behaviourist
position rests.

[2] *The Principle of Individuality and Value* (Macmillan, 1912), iii., iv., v.

[3] Macmillan, 1925.

that of science.   Science itself has no *locus standi* apart from
the spirit of the demand for intelligibility, which drives it
onward in the persons of such thinkers as Mr. Julian Huxley
and Professor Lloyd Morgan to meet the astringent discipline
of critics such as Mr. Joseph, and thus developed to seek a
temporary resting-place in the thought of a Bosanquet or a
Whitehead.   Meanwhile the behaviourist stands outside the
pilgrim throng—and the pity of it is that he has in his hands
a much-needed treasure to contribute to the common wealth
of those who are journeying in the way.

4.  Perhaps the most curious fact of all about the
behaviourist psychology is that it should have come into
vogue just at the time when the cry of the hour in philosophy
is that we should " take time seriously," and recognise the
emergence of real novelties in the history of creation.   To
take but a few names at random, one has only to think of
Bergson, William James, Samuel Alexander and H. Wildon
Carr to be reminded that in all probability the position that
Christian thinkers of the present generation must be prepared
to face is not the denial of all freedom on the basis of a
universal mechanistic predetermination, but the assertion
that God Himself is in process of self-creation, and this with
such freedom that He has not the least idea what He is going
to be or do next.   Such philosophy receives a ready welcome
from many scientists, especially from those biologists, psychologists and sociologists who are emancipating themselves
from the traditional obligation to make their studies conform
to the canons of mathematical physics.   To turn from these
live discussions to the behaviourist contentions seems like
entering an atmosphere curiously antiquated and remote
from the realities of twentieth-century thought.

### III

There is no need to repeat here what has been said
in a previous essay on the importance of psychoanalytic
psychology as calling attention to the purposive character
of many events which occur at a level below that of conscious
individual human intention.[1]   But here again, as in that

---

[1] Above, Essay III.

essay, I would emphasise the contention that to obtain a balanced view of human nature it is necessary to accept and assimilate the contributions of both psychoanalytic and behaviourist schools, uniting them in such a synthesis as that outlined by the late Bernard Bosanquet in the fourth and fifth chapters of "The Principle of Individuality and Value"; and regarding that fount of energy, described variously as *libido*, *élan vital*, life stream, or what not, as the active will of God.   In doing this one ignores the fact that as a general rule the psychoanalyst is professedly as "mechanistic" in his outlook as the behaviourist; he claims to deal with a psychic as distinct from a purely physiological mechanism.   As a result of this many readers of my previous essay would doubtless feel that I had given a misleading account of the psychoanalytic position, which would not be accepted by the average practising psychoanalyst, and that this was hardly a fair way to treat a witness in order to make his evidence support my case.   To this my answer would be that his testimony contained a concealed inconsistency of which he was unaware, and that I had taken the liberty of trying to expound his position in such a way as to make sense of it.   But the point deserves further attention, and to attend to it now will help to set forward the main argument of this essay.

Psychoanalysis took its origin and gained its name in a break-away from the habit of medical science to treat psychology as a branch of physiology.   It was discovered experimentally that certain nervous and mental ills could be relieved, not by rest and bromides, but by exploring their connections with other elements in the "psychic" life of the patient.   The psychoanalyst broke with the traditions of medical practice in thus postulating a "psychic order," a sequence of psychic events distinct from the physical order with which medicine had hitherto concerned itself, and within which it had looked for the causes of both physical and mental ills.   Those who made this discovery had themselves been trained in the traditions from which they revolted, and thus naturally brought with them to their new study and practice many of the ideas with which they had hitherto worked.   They thus transferred to the hypothetical "psychic sequence " the same conception of mechanistic determination to which they had become accustomed in their physiological work.  This seemed to them to be the only way in which they could treat " the new psychology " as scientific and retain their self-respect as scientists.

But what is meant by " psychic " ?  The word seems to be used to describe some kind of non-material substance existing alongside of that other kind of substance called physical.  It is thus akin to the " spiritual substance " of the scholastic philosophers—akin to it in " what it is made of," but differing from it in its habits, being not free but mechanistically determined.  But those of us who have come to disbelieve in the spiritual substance of the scholastics,[1] and to regard the human self or soul as the unifying self-conscious subject of its own bodily experiences, find this " psychic stuff " of the psychoanalysts open to the same criticisms as the " spiritual substance " of the scholastics. The psychoanalytic scheme appears to require an analysis of reality into three kinds of " stuff "—material, psychic, and self-conscious, the psychic being an intermediate grade between the other two.

If for this scheme of three kinds of stuff or substance we substitute the conception of a single cosmic process permeated by an energy which in human bodies becomes aware of itself, and is thus individualised into distinct self-conscious purposive minds, each endowed with some measure of self-determination, we lay bare the confusion latent in psychoanalytic determinism.  We have no room for more than two main divisions : the world of sub-conscious events where we observe from without the behaviour of the permeating energy, and the world of conscious events which we interpret from within as the self-expressions of purposive individuals and the true sphere of value judgments.  The difficulty arises from the fact that, as always in nature, we find the paradox of continuity combined with the emergence of real differences of kind.  In the order of time the world of sub-conscious events precedes the emergence of conscious purposive selves ; in the continuous process wherein the latter come into being

---

[1] See my contribution to *Essays on the Trinity and the Incarnation* (ed. A. E. J. Rawlinson; Longmans, Green & Co., 1928).

on the basis of the bodily organisms developed in the former there is a borderland where the one kind of event shades off into the other as colours shade off into one another when spread out in the spectrum. The behaviourist tries to treat all events as belonging to the earlier order; pan-psychists to treat all as belonging to the second. The psychoanalyst avoids the pitfall of trying to draw a single line to divide the two worlds, but his way of avoiding it is to draw two lines, enclosing a neutral zone to be considered as a third kind of world—as though one were to interpose between red and yellow a third colour which is to be thought of as red in its nature and yellow in its habits.

But why must these events, though " psychic " in nature, be thought of by the psychoanalyst as mechanistic in behaviour? I believe that the answer to this question will carry us far into the heart of our own problem, for I believe that the real urge which underlies the psychologist's demand for a mechanistic subject-matter (rationalise it as he may) is *fear*—fear of finding himself set to deal with a " chancy " universe in which anything may happen anyhow. What he seeks is " dependableness " in the objects of his study, which will make that study a reasonable occupation, and he assumes, without having thought the matter out, that this can only be given by a mechanistic system. But when we do try to think the matter out, and ask ourselves what is the ground of the " dependableness " in the mechanistic order itself, it appears to some of us that we are ultimately driven to find it in what some thinkers would call the plan of the immanent spirit of the whole, and others the will of God.

It is surely in order for the Christian, at this point, to remind his scientific friends that his religion, like their science, has made some progress since primitive magic gave birth to them both. In particular he can call attention to the fact that the Christian religion is characterised by a history peculiarly fitted to meet our present point. As we have noticed already, it was in the early days of primitive Hebrew religion that God was thought of as so unknowable and undependable that man could never have any reasonable idea of what He was going to do next; to find this out he had to cast lots, or have a dream at a sanctuary, or persuade a wizard to peep and mutter. But many centuries before Christ there came that epoch-making assertion of the great prophetic principle that man's moral insight is insight into the will of God.   However faint and fitful may have been the first workings of this principle within the religion of our spiritual ancestors, it was the leaven which was destined to leaven the lump, and its coming was epoch-making just because it contained within it the germ of rational religion.   The moral consciousness of mankind still had much to learn concerning what is good and what evil ;  much still remains to be learned.   But given the principle that insight into the nature of things as revealed in ethics, art, the sciences, philosophy, and history is insight into the character of Him who is the object of our directly personal religious relationships, then our conception of the God we worship will grow *pari passu* with our education in goodness, truth and beauty.   This principle is once for all enshrined in the heart of the Christian religion in the doctrine of the Incarnation, involving as it does the conviction that in the character of the Perfect Man we have revealed to us the character of the God whose will upholds the created universe.   It was a Christian seer who followed the tradition of his Jewish ancestors and chose for His description the epithet " Faithful and True." [1]

For the Christian the goodness of God is the ground of the rationality in the universe in virtue of which man, in his inquiries about it, finds a " dependableness " in its behaviour which makes the inquiry worth pursuing.   The mechanism of the sub-human natural order is itself grounded in the goodness of God ;  because He is faithful and true, and the world of nature carries out His will with untiring and obedient energy, the scientist can safely trust in its uniformity.   But its dependableness as observed is the dependableness of a purely passive uniformity, of a system in which each distinguishable thing carries out willy-nilly the will of the whole.   Men and women are learning what it is to carry out that will as the expression of their own conscious intention.   They are in transit from passive conformity to active co-operation, and on the way they wander off into experiments in self-assertion which run counter to the will of God and introduce that " human element " of uncertainty which is the scientist's despair.

[1] Rev. xix. 2 ;  vi. 10 ;  cp. Dr. Charles's note on iii. 7.

If human life be the opportunity of learning to control the body of which one is made, in accordance with one's glimpses of the will of God, then perfect control—which would be perfect freedom—would be experienced only by one whose apprehension of God's will for him and adoption of it as his own will were perfect. What happens when we assert ourselves as not mere passive things, but in doing so will what is not the will of God for us, either through ignorance or sin ? The problem is very obscure ; but I would tentatively suggest the hypothesis that in so far as our will is other than the will of God we fail to assimilate and control our bodily processes in our spiritual life. The body carries on in a series of events which enter into our awareness, but whose connection with one another is that of the mechanistic system of the bodily life and not that of membership in the consciously organised whole of our spiritual programme. Nevertheless they have entered into our awareness sufficiently to be discoverable through an investigation directed towards associating them as elements in the conscious life, rather than by such an examination of the brain as might conceivably be rendered possible through the perfecting of instruments for a microscopic X-ray examination of it. If this way of thinking about them could be accepted, it would account for the puzzle of their psychological character and their mechanical habits.

Nevertheless, there are difficulties remaining. We have agreed that there can be no room in our scheme of things for any purely " chancy " events—that is, for any events of which no intelligible account can be given exhibiting their place in the coherent scheme of the whole universe. There seem to be two possible ways of giving such an account. The one exhibits the event in its place in the mechanistic sequence of the physical world, as a member of which it has its relevance to the whole scheme. The other exhibits its own intrinsic value as an act which was worth doing. But our acts of ignorance and sin seem to be neither one nor the other. They seem to be essentially unintelligible, having no place either in the mechanistic sequence or in the conscious human fulfilment of the will of God.

May not the truth possibly be that they are indeed unintelligible if taken by themselves, and that the only way to understand them is to regard them as unsuccessful attempts to be something intelligible, unsuccessful attempts to establish themselves as permanently real events. In the divine plan, which is the ultimate principle of intelligibility in the universe, there is given to all men and women a power of conscious self-determination as the condition of their growing into " the glorious liberty of the children of God." [1] They *can* make use of this in such a way as to commit acts which *are* intrinsically irrational and unintelligible, acts which only escape being " surds " in the coherence of the universe because the allowing of them has its place in the divine plan. So far as we can see, that plan includes the eliciting of good human characters through the evolutionary process of creation, and the conception of ready-made good men is self-contradictory in a way that the allowance of the conditions for growth is not. This is not necessarily to minimise the seriousness of sin by treating it merely as a futile mis-shot at goodness. If there be any truth in the Christian doctrine of the Atonement, it should remind us that the freedom allowed us by God is such that we may misuse it in a way which can only be put right by His incarnate suffering and death and our repentance.[2] Sinful acts cannot be fitted into their place in the divine plan, and thus rationalised, by simply *seeing* them in their place in the scheme ; they have to be *put* into their place by divine and human self-sacrifice. Apart from such remaking of them, they come to nothing ; the would-be soul sinks back into the realm of sub-conscious mechanism, from which it might otherwise have emerged to the enjoyment of selfhood, freedom and immortality.

## IV

" There is no smoke without a fire," says the old proverb, and our brief consideration of human nature has shown that both the behaviourist and the psychoanalyst have got hold of something in us that is there to be examined, and that our view of such freedom as we possess must be found in the light of what they have to teach us of the truth about ourselves. The

---

[1] Rom. viii. 21.
[2] See my *And Was Made Man*, chap. v. (Longmans, Green & Co., 1928).

upshot of the discussion, so far, is that we are *in process of becoming free*, but that in order for that process to be possible there does exist what may be called a true freedom of choice, that is to say, a power of self-determination which is controlled neither by external circumstances nor by a man's internal past development as summed up in his character at the moment, but is the power of a free choice of alternatives provided by the fact of his meeting those circumstances with that character. It is only with the greatest reluctance, and after trying every expedient I could think of to avoid it, that I have been driven to recognise the existence of this freedom of choice as a fact in human nature. Generation after generation of philosophers have explained it away, and have pointed out to the plain man that while, indeed, he was right in believing himself to have freedom, that freedom was quite unlike what he imagined it to be, and much more worth having. So I myself have tried to explain it to successive generations of pupils. Those with a natural talent for becoming sophisticated have readily grasped the explanation ; but others have looked puzzled, smiled politely, and (either with or without having asserted that they understood and agreed) have gone away unconvinced.

*Naturam expellas furca, tamen usque recurret* might well be written up as a motto over the doors of a school of philosophy. The history of philosophy is largely the history of attempts to explain away the stubborn facts of nature by describing them in terms of something else which they are not, in order to make them fit into a coherent system which cannot otherwise assimilate them. What if this freedom of choice be such a fact, which has got to be accepted " with natural piety," something which we know perfectly well from the inside through our experience of it, and which just is not adequately described by those philosophical accounts of it which make it out to be other than that which it appears to be and is ?

The necessity of explaining it away arises, of course, from inability otherwise to fit it into the rational coherence of the universe. But if this can be done by viewing it, not as an end in itself, not as that true freedom which is the goal of life, not, indeed, as a possible characteristic of eternal Being, but as a necessary element in the development of creation in time, destined to lose itself in the accomplishment of its task, it may be that by thus " taking time seriously " we shall be able more satisfactorily to weave into our system the witness of the plain man's experience of freedom, his consciousness of a power of choice which may either be lost in slavery to his passions or grow and expand into the true divine freedom, but in either case will be transformed into something other than that which it was to begin with. It is not an ultimately unaccountable element of " chanciness " in the universe ; in so far as there is chance in it, it is like the chance deliberately willed in tossing a coin or holding out two chess pawns in such a way as to preclude any method of determining the course of action to be followed other than guess-work. The contingency is explicable as willed contingency, willed for an intelligible purpose ; and it is such that it cannot be held either to upset the regularity of the mechanistic order or to be ultimately successful in running counter to the will which is the source of existence both to that mechanistic order and to itself.

Once again, as so often, the question of how we can think of the things of this world is found to depend on how we think of God. Shortly after the death of Bernard Bosanquet, Professor C. C. J. Webb delivered in Oxford a commemorative lecture on his Philosophy of Religion, in the course of which he suggested the criticism that Bosanquet had " underrated the importance of the finite individual in the scheme of the universe, or as we may put it in religious language, in the sight of God," [1] and went on to point out the connection between this attitude to the finite individual (revealed in Bosanquet's Gifford Lectures) and the antagonistic attitude later manifested towards the " humanism " of certain thinkers acutely conscious of the importance of the time-process. In his essay on " God and Time," [2] published a few years later, Mr. F. H. Brabant, arguing from the premiss that theology cannot " accept the view according to which God is not God without the Time-process," finds the problem of the relation between God and creation insoluble in so far as what is sought is a

[1] See the *Hibbert Journal*, Oct. 1923 (vol. xxii. p. 90).
[2] In *Essays on the Trinity and the Incarnation* (ed. Rawlinson ; Longmans, Green & Co., 1928).

*metaphysical* ground of that relationship, in the sense of an underlying principle exhibiting the necessity of each to the other. He suggests that the theistic idea of creation, according to which the time-space universe springs from the *will* of God, after a manner pictured by moral rather than metaphysical analogies, enables us more adequately to assimilate and reconcile the various factors which enter into the problem of time and eternity. Without doubt the inspiration one never fails to draw from the study of Bosanquet's works is due in great part to the gallant enthusiasm with which he devoted himself to the search for a metaphysical solution of the problem, and the sincere thoroughness with which he worked out his suggestion towards that end, exhibiting its implications in detail, and accepting them with unflinching steadfastness. Nevertheless, if his work is justly criticised by Professor Webb (as I, for my part, think it is), it is because here in this time-space world of ours there *are* a contingency and a freedom of choice which cannot be given their due place in his system. He has described admirably the freedom to which we aspire, the only kind of freedom we really want ; but he cannot do justice to that other freedom, which (though it has to lose itself in its fulfilment) is a necessary condition of our aspiring. Because the time-process is seen as God's self-manifestation through a creation which is, as it were, the eternal reality strung out in time and space, and not a relatively independent order struggling towards its goal, and incapable of being reconciled in thought with the demands of reason until it has been reconciled in deed with the demands of goodness, he cannot admit the temporal reality of a freedom which is eternally inexplicable. But from age to age the Christian faith has resolutely reaffirmed its determination to hold fast to both sides of the problem and to endure the consequent tension until a solution shall be found capable of doing justice in both directions, bearing witness to the temporal reality of time and the relative independence of the temporal order by its use of the word " creation," and affirming in the doctrine of the Blessed Trinity the intrinsic perfection of the divine Life, the source and ground of all created existence, itself neither enriched by creation's progress nor impoverished by its disasters, seeing that from that same Godhead come both the riches wherewith creation is blessed and the love whereby its sins are redeemed.

We have travelled some distance, round and round about, since we left Dr. Jowett and his undergraduate. The tour will have been worth while if it has enabled us to see a little more clearly what is involved in asserting, with the Master, our belief in human freedom. It would be folly to make any claim to be able to demonstrate the existence of our freedom; but we have, perhaps, made some progress towards envisaging the kind of world-order in which it could be given an intelligible place.

In our present condition we are in process of transition from functioning willy-nilly in the mechanistic order towards a full co-operative sharing in the perfect freedom of God. In a large measure the behaviourist is right when he says that we are not free, for behaviouristic functioning still plays a large part in our life—larger, perhaps, than we commonly realise. If it were not so, behaviourist psychology would not hold the place of honour which it does in schools where advertisers and salesmen are trained; nor would a priest have to face the temptation to substitute for the more difficult task of eliciting their free response to the love of God the easier method of conditioning his flock to go through the motions of worship. We are still in part mechanistic, but we are also in part free. And yet our freedom is far from perfect—so far, indeed, that it is, *as it stands*, intrinsically unintelligible! It exists only to be either transformed or lost, and it can be fitted into a scheme of the universe only if in that scheme sufficient reality is ascribed to the time-process to allow of its containing elements intelligible as temporal realities, but untranslatable into terms of eternal being except by actual transformation: temporary irrationalities within a rational scheme analogous to the tossing of a coin as an expression of the spirit of fairness in sport.

We must not, then, be surprised or put out when our behaviourist friend shows us that in some action of ours we were not as free as we had thought we were. Maybe he is right. We do not assert that in every action of ours we are partially free, nor that in any action we are wholly free. But it is our faith and hope that some day, please God, we shall be;

and in spite of our philosophical and psychological friends we refuse to explain away that odd and self-contradictory experience of freedom here and now which is the earnest of our hope.

A few years ago a theological student, shortly to be ordained, told a friend that he had come to the conclusion that there was no such thing as unselfishness. He said that he had been examining his past life in preparation for his ordination, and that on reflection he could not honestly say that he had ever done a really unselfish act. Looking back over his life he could see in all his acts, even in those he had thought best and most unselfish at the time, the slimy trail of the serpent of selfishness. His friend, after a caution against overscrupulosity and cynicism, suggested that the existence of unselfishness does not depend on its perfect expression in any one of us up to date, and recalled the saying of the saint that if his self-love died twenty minutes before he did he would sing "Nunc Dimittis." But did he mean to assert that the same serpentine trail was to be found in the life of Christ, and that selfishness had a home in the social life of the Blessed Trinity?

As with unselfishness, so with freedom. Our freedom is inchoate, imperfect and irrational. If freedom such as ours were asserted of God, then the scientist might indeed throw up his hands at the prospect of facing a "chancy" universe. But behind all is the perfect freedom of God, perfectly informed by His goodness, the rational ground of the "dependableness" discovered in the natural order, the ground of our hope that one day we too shall attain to the glorious liberty of the sons of God.

## V. FREEDOM, GRACE AND PROVIDENCE

UNLESS he has allowed himself to be sophisticated into denying his convictions, the Christian is apt to find himself a genuine Mr. Facing-both-ways on the subject of freedom. Confronted by a behaviourist, he strictly maintains that he is really free to initiate action; confronted by a Pelagian, he asserts with equal vehemence the necessity of divine grace, and acknowledges the truth of his Master's words : " Apart from me ye can do nothing." How can these things be ?

" In our present condition we are in process of transition from functioning willy-nilly in the mechanistic order towards a full co-operative sharing in the perfect freedom of God." The answer to the question is to be found, I believe, by working out the implications of this view of human life.

I

The last essay, from which the above statement is quoted, was an attempt at working out some of those implications, with especial reference to the relation of human life to that mechanistic order from which it emerges. The aim there was to establish the first of the two Christian convictions about freedom. The aim of this essay is to deal with the second, and to consider freedom in relation to our fellow-men and to God. But there are one or two further points concerning our relation to our sub-human environment which it is necessary to notice before we pass on.

In the previous essay we were chiefly concerned to notice the difference between events expressing human volition and events in the mechanistic order, and to advocate a view of human life in which the keynote is sympathy with the struggles of men and women to extricate themselves from the trammels of their original nature and attain to the glorious liberty of the sons of God. The mechanistic sequence of cause and effect appeared as an enemy of our freedom, offering dangerously seductive inducements to us to refuse the responsibility of our inchoate selfhood and to let ourselves be carried along in the stream of events. But we must not forget that this very regularity and orderliness becomes not the hindrance but the help to our self-expression, when once we make the venture of setting out to discover what we can be and do. If I never knew whether the result of putting a kettle on the fire would be to boil the water in it or to freeze it, it would not be much good deciding to make myself a cup of tea. The progressive conquest of nature through scientific discovery, on the principle that " Nature is conquered by being obeyed," is simply the methodical extension of everyone's experience, an extension which discovers new possibilities of human self-expression. Thus the orderliness of nature, which is due to its being informed by the good will of God, crowns its habit of producing novelties by producing beings capable of taking an intelligent share in the work, to whom it presents itself as material adapted to their needs. To enter into knowledge of its ways is to enter into God's mind ; to learn to distinguish its right from its wrong use is also to enter into God's mind. Both methods need to be combined if man's relation to the physical world is to promote his growth in freedom. Poison gas is not always employed in the cause of liberty.

Thus man comes to take a co-operative hand in the process whereby he is himself being created. In that process real novelties do occur ; so long as we limit our view to the world of time and space it is not true to say " Ex nihilo nil fit." The successive stages of evolution, and human inventions, are all evidences of such novelties. The difference between those in the production of which man has had a hand and those in which he has not is, so far as we can see, simply that fact itself. In the former case the time-space order functions passively ; in the latter individuals belonging to that order are expressing themselves as conscious purposive contributors to the story.

Once again it must be remembered that in nature we

cannot draw clear-cut lines to make boundaries. It is difficult in these days to say anything about the difference between human beings and sub-human nature without someone in the audience getting up to say that he knows a horse that can count or a hen that can do something or other of the same kind. This is quite beside the point. The transition from passive functioning to active co-operation may be a very slow and gradual development, and the points we select as marking distinct stages may be as arbitrary as the action of a father when he says to his son : " You may do so and so when you are twelve years old," or of the law which fixes the date for " coming-of-age." Nevertheless there are very real differences between babyhood, boyhood and maturity. Now in the case before us, it might be possible to distinguish many different stages in the development, and for the purposes of other inquiries it might be necessary to do so. But for our purpose it is sufficient to distinguish between passive functioning (however far back lies the last pure instance of it) and active co-operation (however far ahead lies the full realisation of it).

It is argued by the behaviourist that the right way to obtain a true understanding of human activity is to view it from without as a detached observer. A human community thus viewed, he claims, appears just like an ant-heap or bee-hive. Why should we desire to think of them as any different ? We should, I think, agree that he is right in holding that the two communities would look alike to the outside observer, adding that in our opinion the better the human community the more it would resemble the ants and bees. Nor should we deny the value of trying to view human life in this way ; but we should point out that if we confine ourselves to this observation *ab extra*, we run the risk of missing the point of the process we are observing. Human society is in process of transition from functioning as a behaviouristic herd to the free co-operative activity of a truly social community. From the outside we might be able to notice the ordered dovetailing of the individual activities in the herd, the disorderly maladjustments of the intermediate stages, and the regained order of the City of God. But only from within can we find the interpretation of the story, and know the significance of the changes through which creation is wrought out in time.

As was said above, there is no need, for the purpose of this essay, to inquire closely about the extent to which progress has been made on the journey in various forms of animal life. Our point is that *in so far as* the individual member of a herd lacks full conscious awareness of the part it is playing in the social whole, and *in so far as* that part is not his own consciously given contribution, his movements are behaviouristically conditioned and controlled. Now it is characteristic of this behaviouristic mode of functioning that the individual is moved as it were from without, by an external force which pushes and pulls it along willy-nilly. At this level of behaviour there is no individual freedom, and everything is moved by the necessity of an external physical compulsion. Individual freedom begins when the individual, already so moved to conform with the movements of his fellows, becomes aware of the fact and able to carry on or contract out. Social co-operation is the voluntary co-operation of individuals consciously working for a common end. The secret of human life is to learn to pass from being externally [1] compelled to function as one of the herd to being internally moved to free co-operation with society.

We can see this process recapitulated in every generation. The relation of parents to children is one in which it is (or should be) exhibited. No matter how great the love of the parent for the child, it must at first be moved externally and treated as a little machine. It has to be lifted from place to place, and stays where it is put. It has to be physically fed and otherwise attended to, and the more mechanically regular the routine, the better the results. But as the years go by, the external physical control of parent over child grows less

---

[1] The words " externally " and " internally " are used for convenience and for want of better ones. It is not, of course, the localisation in space of the origin of the movement which is in question, but the degree in which it is the activity of a " self." In the events of levels where there is nothing to be called a self at all, it is clearly absurd to speak of that " self " being moved either from within or without. Where selfhood has begun to emerge, the developing self may be moved partially behaviouristically and partially freely. In so far as it functions behaviouristically I speak of it as " moved externally," even though the seat of the motion be within its organic constitution ; in so far as it acts freely I speak of it as " moved internally," even though it be moving in response to the call of love from without.

and less, and all being well it passes over into a mutual understanding wherein son is proud of father and father of son, but neither thinks of trying to coerce the other into agreement with him.

If we " take time seriously " and recognise the coming into existence of novelties which may possibly behave in ways unlike those of previously existing things, we need not be surprised to find at the level of true social co-operation modes of personal intercommunion previously unexampled in the physical world. It is possible for the influence of one man's life on that of another to give him real help, and yet not to diminish but rather to increase his freedom. The influence of Brown over Jones may be such that the latter can say quite truly to Robinson : " But for Brown I could not be what I am," and can with equal truth repudiate the suggestion that Brown's influence has in any way diminished his own freedom. " On the contrary," he might say, " I am conscious of being the more free as a result of the help he has given me, and it is for this that I am especially grateful to him."

The first necessity for our thinking is that we should recognise this fact as a fact. It is time to emancipate ourselves from the hypnotic influence of the nineteenth century, which forbids us to accept as facts whatever cannot be " explained " in terms of physical necessity. Let it be that at lower levels of behaviour external compulsion and internal freedom are contradictory, the one to the other. We are aware in our own experience that this is not always so in human relationships, and as believers in the temporal reality of time we claim the right to compare spiritual things with spiritual. *At our level of experience* external help and internal freedom may be the obverse and reverse sides of a single process.

Nor is this fact simply a brute unintelligible fact. The conception of a co-operative society of free beings is an intelligible conception, and a worthy object of creation for a Creator worthy of our worship. Unless, therefore, each man's inchoate freedom were to be developed by God in isolated independence from that of his fellows, there must emerge, at some stage or other in the creative process, just such mutual helpfulness as will promote and not hinder growth in freedom. It was argued in the last essay that freedom as we have it now must pass away, either by sinking out of existence into the mechanistic order from which it sprang, or by rising into its consummation as the perfect freedom which " cannot sin." Growth in the inner freedom of self-control and moral achievement may change the nature of our freedom, but it changes it by perfecting it, not by destroying it; and any aid from others which would help onward that growth would be intelligible as an element entering into a complex social fact, consistent with the free response which it evoked. The facts observed at our level of experience are such as to encourage us to believe that this is the method actually germane to God's plan of creation, and, so interpreted, themselves appear somewhat less brutish.

It is clear that such thinkers as Professor Webb and Dr. John Oman are right when they suggest that it is along the lines of considerations such as these that we must approach the subject of God's grace.[1] " Grace " is the technical term for that divine help which enables a man to be and do what otherwise would be impossible for him. The danger to be avoided is that of regarding grace as a " something " detachable from God's living personal activity, and capable of working on its own as a kind of impersonal deputy for God—like the dictaphone which repeats a man's letters to his typist after he has gone out to play golf, or the medicine which helps a patient between the doctor's visits. It has been well remarked that such interposition of a mediating " thing " in the relations of God and man represents a degradation of religion, and is a mark of its having succumbed to a standing temptation against which all religions need to be on their guard. " God's grace " is God in action regarded under the aspect of Helper, as God's love is God in action regarded under the aspect of Lover. His grace can no more be " reified " (as McDougall would say) than His love. The language of devotion which seems to imply that it can is best interpreted by reference to the language of letter-writing according to which we are frequently sending love by post. " With my love " means " I love you." " My

---

[1] See Webb: *Problems in the Relation of God and Man* (London, Nisbet, 1911); Oman: *Grace and Personality* (Cambridge University Press, 1919).

grace is sufficient for thee " means " He that abideth in me, and I in him, the same beareth much fruit : for apart from me ye can do nothing." [1]

As in the personal relations between man and man, so, too, in the personal relations between God and man, God can really help and man be really helped, and yet there need be no setting aside of the man's freedom.   Moreover, there is, as a matter of fact, less danger of God's grace interfering with human freedom than of man's influence.   There *is* a way of influencing to action which *does* constrict freedom, and we are often tempted to use it in the wrong place.[2]   But God may be trusted never to misuse it.   It is intriguing to notice on reflection that the truth about intercessory prayer is just the opposite of popular opinion.   There is nothing more irritating than to be told by a pious friend who has failed in open argument or exhortation : " Well, good-bye— I'll pray for you."   You feel that he is going to try to " get at " you by underhand means and influence you against your will when off your guard.   But consider the matter from the other side.   Imagine yourself possessed by the desire to prevail upon a man to do something, fully realising, however, that unless he did it of his own will it were better that he should not do it at all.   Imagine yourself anxious lest there be anything in the alleged facts of telepathy which might give you a power of " getting at " him when off his guard. What greater safeguard could there be against this danger than to turn to God, putting the whole matter into the hands of One who may be relied upon not to insinuate into your friend's life any influence inconsistent with his growth in freedom ?

The love-potion, whereby in " A Midsummer Night's Dream " Titania was induced to fall in love with ass-headed Bottom, reflects, without doubt, a popular belief of Shakespeare's day according to which love could be won by such means.   To-day a young man who wished to woo a girl, and thought to do so by going to a drug store to buy a powder to be slipped in her tea when she was not looking, would rightly be thought a lunatic.   We need to be careful not to retain in our religious thinking notions which we have

---

[1] John xv. 5.          [2] See above, p. 42; below, p. 62.

abandoned elsewhere. If once upon a time love-potions were ever accepted instruments in human social intercourse, it may have been justifiable to think of sacraments after their analogy. There is no justification for such an approach to the subject of sacramental grace to-day.[1]

Why should we ever feel a desire for such an approach? Two factors, I believe, combine to lead us into this temptation. The lingering influence of the outlook inherited from days when love-philtres were intellectually *comme il faut* unites with the nineteenth-century habit of finding in the mechanistic sequence of cause and effect the true home of *dependable* activity. Thus an illustration, based on the nineteenth-century outlook, whereby the sureness of sacramental grace is likened to the flowing of water or electric current from reservoir through appointed channels to where it is needed to nourish or empower, is in danger of speaking home to that in us which still would fain live in a world of love-philtres. We need to meditate on the true nature of our relations with our fellow-men, and on the truth that the goodness of God is the ground of His " dependability." We need to meditate on the difference between being drawn by love and driven by drugs. We need to remember that the Eucharist is the meeting-place of living Christians with living Christ, and its grace the power that comes into human life through personal communion with such a Person. We shall not go wrong if we follow that strain in St. Augustine's teaching wherein the grace of God is defined as the love of God spread abroad in our hearts by the Holy Spirit, whereby we cry " Abba, Father! "[2] St. Paul went to the heart of the doctrine of grace when he said " The love of Christ constraineth us." [3]

II

The difficulties of the notion of Providence are notorious. The word is a religious word, and it expresses the religious man's faith that God watches over his ways and the ways of all creation, guiding the course of events in accordance with

---

[1] On this subject, see further, below, Essay IX.
[2] Cp. *De Spiritu et Littera*, passim.
[3] 2 Cor. v. 14.

His will.  So he prays that we may " do all such good works as thou hast prepared for us to walk in," and regards the situations in which he finds himself as " meant."  Nevertheless, he clings to the conviction that many acts of his own and of his fellow-men, which have gone to the making of this " meant" situation, were free, were unpredictable until they were done, and in some cases were contrary to the will of God.  How can this freedom be reconciled with God's providential care?  How can foreknowledge be consistent with contingency?

Quite apart from the particular colour given to the problem through its religious associations, wherein it receives the name of Providence, the question of temporal contingency in relation to eternal determinateness provides (as was seen more than once in the last essay) serious problems for secular philosophy.  It is curious but true that, while this problem drives secular philosophy into religion in search of its solution, religion appears inhospitably to sharpen the difficulties rather than to remove them.  To add the words " foreknown " and " preordained " to the impersonal " predetermined " seems but to hammer down the nails in the coffin of contingency.  It is in its theological form that the question must ultimately be faced.

Nevertheless, it will be well to begin with the problem of secular philosophy, the problem of contingency.  The denial of contingency springs from accepting the principle that " the rational is the real," and interpreting it as meaning that whatever is irrational is really, *here and now*, something other than what it appears to be.  The apparent mistake must be really the expression of " an unconscious purpose " [1]; the apparently free act must be really the appropriate response of the organism to its environment.  There is nothing which is not what it necessarily must be : otherwise it would be a " surd " in the system, the system would be irrational, and all thought would be impossible—

> " Were it not better done as others use,
>     To sport with *Amaryllis* in the shade,
>     Or with the tangles of *Neæra's* hair ? "

[1] Cp. Freud : *General Introduction to Psychoanalysis* (New York : Boni & Liveright, 1920), Lecture II.

So dominant had the conviction become that whatever is necessarily must be so, that when at last the reaction against absolute idealism set in, and our attention was recalled to the duty of recognising such things as novelties in time, contingency, and " brute facts " as being what they are, there was need of exhibiting fallacious arguments whose fallacy was due to this conviction lurking unnoticed in the process of thought.   In Oxford, the late Professor Cook Wilson used to examine the argument that " If $x$ will happen to-morrow, it must be true to-day that $x$ will happen to-morrow : therefore it must be determined to-day that $x$ will happen to-morrow." He used to point out that this argument involves a confusion between two statements : (*a*) " It is true to-day that what will happen, will happen "; and (*b*) "Circumstances exist to-day which necessitate $x$ happening to-morrow."   The first statement—which is all that we are justified in making—signifies nothing *ad rem, unless we identify it with the second*, and to do this is to beg the very question at issue.   At Cambridge Mr. G. E. Moore has exhibited a similar fallacy, showing that an inability to recognise the existence of " mere matters of fact " has led to a confusion between " is now as a matter of fact " and " must necessarily be." [1]   The mistake, the mere matter of fact, the contingent event—these all exist in time and space ; how are they to be accounted for ?   If this spatio-temporal order of events is to be regarded as the self-manifestation of a rational reality, they *must* be explained away as in some sense unreal, and unreal here and now, as things which will turn out to be other than they appear when seen in the light of that eternal whole of which they are the partial manifestation.

It is the contention of certain thinkers to-day, notably Mr. A. N. Whitehead and Mr. Paul Elmer More (if I understand them rightly), that the universe is rational, but that its rationality is communicated to it by a God who Himself is the non-rational ground of the universal rationality. [2]   In this they bear witness to what I believe to be true, that it is impossible to regard as rational both the here-and-now spatio-temporal order, and the eternal reality in which it is grounded.

[1] *Philosophical Studies* (London, 1922), X, on " External and Internal Relations."

[2] Cp. Whitehead : *Science in the Modern World* (New York, 1925), pp. 249–251 ; More : *Christ the Word* (Princeton, 1927), chaps. iii. and iv.

But I venture to think that they are mistaken in their opinion as to which of the two it is that is rational ; that in truth it is the eternal reality which alone is through and through rational and thus intelligible, and that no philosophical system can exhibit this spatio-temporal universe as it stands as being rational and intelligible, because as it stands it is not so. Nevertheless, it is not unreal in the sense that it is a world of appearances which can be thought away ; it is real with what may perhaps be called the temporal mode of reality as contrasted with the eternal.    What is meant by the temporal mode of reality is that it is a process which has to be worked out in time before it can be thought through in the light of eternity and found intelligible.

But how can the rational eternal reality communicate to the spatio-temporal process a mode of reality which can pass through stages involving the existence of irrational elements ? It is this question which drives philosophy to religion for its answer, for (as was argued in the last essay) it is in the carrying out of rational acts of will, intelligible on the ground of their intrinsic value *as a whole*, that we find within our experience a place for contingency, for events intrinsically irrational but explicable as means towards the achieving of the intelligible end.    It is thus by finding intelligent and intelligible personality in God, and regarding the spatio-temporal process as due to His *will*, that we can understand in some measure the function of those irrational events which are temporarily real and yet incapable of being established in eternity until transformed in time.    To allow for this the Christian faith suggests the use of the metaphor " creation " to describe the relation between God and the spatio-temporal universe, the metaphor best suited to emphasise both the independence of the universe as spatio-temporal reality, and also its dependence on the will of the Eternal.[1]

But now, as we have seen, our particular difficulty is sharpened, for when we think of the eternal reality as Eternal God, we must think of Him as eternally knowing the whole time-process, and eternally energising every moment of

---

[1] On this whole subject see Mr. C. C. J. Webb's Gifford Lectures : *God and Personality* and *Divine Personality and Human Life* (London, 1918 and 1920), as well as Mr. Brabant's essay on *God and Time*, referred to on p. 40 above.

actuality on earth. With God omniscient and omnipotent, how can we avoid regarding the divine power and knowledge as inconsistent with earthly contingency?

The question whether God knows the details of the contingent is, of course, no new one. But it seems possible that our growing apprehension of what it means to " take time seriously " may throw some light upon it. If it means that we must regard the spatio-temporal universe as a sphere of reality within which contingent events and mere matters of fact have a true share in what we have called the temporal mode of reality, then this belief will have its implications for our conception of God. For if what we are asserting is the temporal reality of the essentially unknowable, then it must be unknowable for God as well as for man. And it is just precisely this which is asserted. The absolute-idealist criticism of contingency was on the ground that nothing opaque to thought can be real; we have found ourselves driven to assert that there is a mode of reality open to things opaque to thought. It was of the essence of the argument that these things are not opaque to thought merely because seen from a finite standpoint in time, but intrinsically. They cannot be understood by being *seen* in the light of eternity, or as God sees them. They are not, here and now, really different from what they appear to be. They are what they are, and have to be *made* different before they can be seen as different. And if what they are is irrational, they are intrinsically unknowable, whether God or man be the would-be knower. To assert that God knows the contingent or the " mere matter of fact " is in fact to deny that they are what they are, *to deny their existence as truly contingent or truly " mere matter of fact,"* to argue an idealist position which underestimates the reality of time. If God's creative activity include the creation of contingent events, that means the creation of events opaque to His thought; this is one element in the Divine self-limitation involved in His creative activity.[1] God as well as man must " take time seriously."

But what then becomes of the religious demand for divine

[1] In *Essays on the Trinity and the Incarnation* (ed. Rawlinson; Longmans, 1928) I have tried to show how this doctrine of God's self-limitation in creation is the necessary basis of the doctrine of the Incarnation.

providential control over the events of human life in this
world ?  What of the religious interpretation of situations as
" meant " ?  To find an answer to these questions we must
examine the ideas of providence and predestination directly
from the religious point of view.

### III

The thought of predestination as meaning an arbitrary
divine destining of certain men to eternal bliss and of certain
others to eternal perdition, despite the prominent part it has
played in the history of Christian thinking, need only be
mentioned in order to be dismissed.  Down at the roots of
true religion, whether it be social or individual, there would
seem to lie a conviction of being chosen or called by God.
This brings with it the temptation to answer the question
" *Why* am I called ? " by " For my own benefit as contrasted
with others," instead of by " For the glory and service of
God." [1]  Against the tendency to fall into this temptation on
the part of the chosen people prophet after prophet has left his
protests on record in the pages of the Old Testament.  Our
Lord still had to struggle with it in the days of His flesh, and
the inability of the chosen people in His time to rise out of it
was one of the chief reasons why official Judaism broke in
His hand as an instrument for the setting up of the true
Messianic Kingdom.  Among the evil fruits of surrender to
this temptation are morbid preoccupation with questions of
soteriology, the thought of the Church as the Ark of Salvation,[2] and the theory of predestination to eternal salvation or
damnation.

Nevertheless the word " predestination " conveys to the
religious mind an ineluctable truth.  Apart from the question
of how we interpret the purpose of our calling, the fact remains
that no one of us, if he be honest, can ascribe his membership in the fellowship of Christ's Church entirely to his own
agency.  It was not of my doing that I was born of a Christian
family in England and brought up in the Christian faith, so

---

[1] On this subject see Dean Armitage Robinson's *Exposition* of Ephesians i.
(Macmillan, 1909).
[2] On this see below, Essay XI, pp. 138–140.

that when I became aware of myself I found myself an English Christian and not a Caribbean Voodooist or a Chinese Confucian. Nor can the man whose Christianity is due to an act of conscious adherence to the faith claim to have directed the circumstances which led to his hearing the Gospel. In one way or another our religion has come to us rather than we to it ; that is why we think of ourselves as called or chosen, and in thinking of ourselves as called or chosen we ascribe to God an activity anticipating in time our response to it. It was " in God's providence " that we were called to the knowledge of His grace and faith in Him. If the word " predestination " means anything, it means the conviction that God in His providence has a purpose or destiny for us which we discover rather than create. From moment to moment our lives are in His hand. The situations in which we find ourselves are " meant," and it is for us to discover their meaning, which is God's meaning. This is the religious interpretation of life. How can it be the true one ?

The thought of God as a kind of celestial chess-player moving His pieces about on the surface of the earth is adequate neither for science, philosophy nor religion. Religion, as was pointed out at the very beginning of this essay, insists that man has more freedom than a pawn even while insisting that his time is in God's hand.

If our previous argument may be trusted, we have discovered two modes in which God does actually enter into and control the course of events in this world of time and space. In the physical order His control is absolute and what we call mechanistic. The " uniformity of nature " reflects the fulfilment of the will of God through passive matter. In human life the control is by grace, and is thus conditioned by that condition intrinsic to God's creative purpose, the purpose of creating free beings to co-operate with Him and respond to His love.[1] Every event which occurs in human life occurs as a result of the interaction of these three factors, natural law, human freedom and divine grace, and it is *within this interaction* that God's providence must be thought of as operative.

---

[1] It should not be necessary again to point out that this distinction is not invalidated by the recognition of intermediate stages in which it may be difficult to discover which element is the more prominent.

The spatio-temporal universe as a whole owes its existence to God's will and depends upon Him, but He has made it *as it is*, and to control the course of events within the system he enters in and works in accordance with the nature of that process *as He has made it*. It contains mere matters of fact, contingency, unpredictable events. He has made it so, and is without repentance. But He comes within and from the inexhaustible resources of His omnipotence triumphs over every possible obstacle to the completion of His plan.

Within the spatio-temporal universe the form taken by God's omnipotence is the power to rise above all circumstances and to turn them to good account, to make them minister to the fulfilment of His will. The classical example of this is, of course, the Cross. Sin's triumph turns out to be God's victory, and the day of crucifixion is celebrated throughout the Christian world as *Good* Friday. The Christian life is a life based on a venture of faith : " No circumstances are too much for God, therefore no circumstances are too much for me if I walk through life hand in hand with God." Conviction of the truth of the Christian view of life comes from making this venture of faith and verifying it in experience. But it is our part here to reflect upon it in thought.

Once again, the question at issue is of what it means to " take time seriously." Reasons have been given for suggesting that it means regarding this universe as containing realities which, being as they stand irrational and unintelligible, have to be *made* different before they can be seen differently and so truly known. We are in the midst of a creative process, surrounded by raw materials to be used in its further continuance. What is it that is in process of being created ? The Christian hypothesis is that it is a society of finite individual beings each perfectly free and all united in perfect voluntary co-operation. The Christian claim is that the acceptance of this hypothesis enables us, as no other hypothesis does, to find some meaning in the given facts of scientific, historical and personal experience without having to resort to distorting them or explaining them away.

The very heart of the matter is the question of freedom. If what God really cares about above all things is the eliciting of perfect freedom, and if the manner of its eliciting be that which I have tried to describe in the last essay and this one, then His purpose demands that His control shall be a control which is consistent with it. The plan demands that when creation arrives at the human level, there shall " emerge " individual self-conscious beings who shall have a hand in their own making and in that of society. At that level God continues to elicit true freedom by the help of His grace. But as true freedom is only to be won through moral progress, man has the choice either by co-operation with God to become a rational being capable of the eternal mode of reality, or to sink back into the impersonal mechanistic order from which he has come. The future is in process of creation, and men are fellow-workers with God in the process. That which is made capable of partaking in the eternal mode of reality will endure ; that which is made otherwise will pass away.

On the basis of this position we may attempt to interpret what the religious man means when he regards a given situation as " meant." Every situation is an opportunity for further creative activity in co-operation with God ; in every situation God has a meaning for us to find, but it can only be found in the activity of making it come true. Life comes to us as plastic raw material, not as finished product, and it has to be fashioned before it can be understood. It is the raw material out of which spiritual realities are to be created. The spirit is not an alien kind of " stuff " imprisoned in the material ; in this world the spatio-temporal realities are the stuff of which the spiritual life is in process of being made. As a sculptor might see that a certain piece of marble was " just asking to " be made into a certain kind of statue, so the man whose life is lived in communion with God might see that a certain situation was " just asking to " be treated as the raw material for the creation of a certain kind of spiritual reality.

There is a story of a man who prayed earnestly one morning for grace to overcome his besetting sin of impatience. A little later he missed a train by half a minute and spent an hour stamping up and down the station platform in furious vexation. Five minutes before the next train came in he suddenly realised that here had been the answer to his prayer.

He had been given an hour to practise the virtue of patience ; he had missed the opportunity and wasted the hour.    There are also many stories of men who have similarly missed trains which have been wrecked, and who ascribe their escape to Providence.    If they are combining the thought of God as the celestial chess-player with the thought of God as pre-eminently concerned in their enjoyment of earthly life at the expense of others, there is not much to be said for their point of view. But if they are humbly acknowledging a call to further service on earth before they pass beyond, they are rightly interpreting their escape.    In all probability all the events which led up to all these men missing their various trains could be adequately accounted for in terms of the interaction of natural law, human freedom and divine grace.    But at every point within that interaction God sees what are its possibilities for good, and the man who shares His enlightenment and His power and gives himself to make that good come true, has found the meaning of that moment and his " special providence." The gates of the future are indeed open, the universe is in the making.    But only if made aright can the making stand. To make it awry may delay the final consummation, but God has no need of hurry.    It is to the quality of the developed freedom that He looks, and He grudges no time in its creation. The end is sure, for He who at every moment in the process sees its possibilities for good is God omnipotent—omnipotent to turn all circumstances to good account, to turn to-day's defeat into to-morrow's victory.    But this omnipotence will never be so exercised as to substitute the external compulsion of men for the internal eliciting of their freedom.    It is freedom that is being created, and by the conditions of its creation its Creator abides.

I have tried elsewhere [1] to show how the recognition of this plastic quality of life, considered with reference to the crucial instance of pain, throws light on the problems of forgiveness and atonement ; and I shall have something more to say about it in the next essay.

There is perhaps no finer description of the religious attitude to life than the words of de Musset : " Les douleurs passagères blasphèment et accusent le ciel ; les grandes

---

[1] *And Was Made Man*, chap. v.

douleurs n'accusent ni le blasphèment, elles écoutent." It is the " listening " attitude which finds the meaning. This discussion of Providence began by asking whether the idea of Providence tenable in accordance with our philosophy would be recognisable as that implied in the religious man's convictions. I would like to end it by asking whether the true basis of these convictions is not the experience of those who have seized the opportunity, redeemed the time, and thereby found the meaning? It is these men and women who, looking backwards, see that the thing was " meant." Others, realising too late that they had missed the moment of opportunity, may with equal truth lament the fact that there was a meaning they had failed to grasp—asserting by that phrase just the very plasticity of the future for which I am contending. *Fronte capillata est, post est occasio calva.* Superstitious parodies of this truly religious trust in God provide us with no obligation to attempt their philosophical justification.

## IV

To regard the eliciting of true finite freedom through the process necessary for its perfection as the purpose of creation suggests certain practical considerations which are worthy of attention. Embedded in the course of the discussion throughout this essay and the last are six fundamental tenets which may now be summarised :

1. Personal goodness, whether of God or man, is nothing but *free* self-expression in acts either themselves intrinsically worth while or contributory to what is intrinsically worth while.[1]

2. The performance of such acts on the part of man tends to promote his growth in freedom ; the performance of contrary acts tends to hinder it.

3. An act may be deficient in either (*a*) voluntariness, or (*b*) the quality of being worth while ; that is to say (*a*) the right thing may be done, but done for some other reason than the free choice of it, or (*b*) the wrong thing may be done of free choice.

[1] See Essay VI, below, for a discussion of what is meant by " worth while."

4. Man is in process of emerging from a state of passive conformity with the immanent energy of the universe, through a state of becoming aware of what is going on and of himself as a potential co-operator in the process, into the actualisation of that potentiality. In this middle stage he has to develop his freedom by asserting it in the creation of what is worth while. If he fails either (a) to assert it at all, or (b) to assert it in the right direction, he fails in one of two mutually complementary necessities.

5. A man's environment at the human stage of his development consists of (i) created nature continuing to function at the levels from which he has emerged ; (ii) other human beings like unto himself ; and (iii) God. Towards (i) a man's attitude may be that of exercising external control ; towards (ii) it should be that of developing personal relationships and eliciting freedom ; towards (iii) it should be that of personal loving self-devotion.

6. God offers to man, in his relationship with (i) and (ii), the opportunity of playing a co-operative part in the work of creation.

If these tenets be accepted as well grounded in a reasonable interpretation of the universe, then it is clear that great practical problems arise in connection with numbers three, four and five.

In considering that relationship between man and man which we described as " influence," we distinguished between the power one man has of externally " conditioning " another after the manner advocated by the behaviourists, and the power of " internally " helping him by developed personal intercourse. Without doubt there is a standing temptation to all men who are interested in reforming, improving, or uplifting their fellows to adopt the more immediately easy method of the behaviourist and to forget the worthlessness of any priestcraft which fails to be true to St. Paul's principle : " We have renounced the hidden things of dishonesty, not walking in craftiness, nor handling the word of God deceitfully ; but by manifestation of the truth commending ourselves to every man's conscience in the sight of God." [1] We have to remember, for instance, that our conduct of

[1] 2 Cor. iv. 2.

public worship must aim at eliciting every worshipper's free conscious self-devotion to God rather than at conditioning him by means of external surroundings to go through the emotional motions of worship and nothing more. From this we might hastily conclude that such external conditioning is always wrong, that the puritan director of worship is right in insisting that if a man shall not worship in the most unhelpful conditions he shall not worship at all, and that we must live continually in the spirit of the man who prays lest his will should influence that of his fellow-men in any other way than that of consciously received influence. But the problem of life is not so simple as this.

We have seen how in the relationship of parents to children the mode of intercourse should pass by gradual and often imperceptible stages from that of " external " control to that of " internal " help. Almost every variety of influence between the two extremes may have its right exercise at the appropriate stage. But this is true not only in this particular relationship, but in many others. For there are men and women who represent every conceivable stage in the development from behaviourist functioning to free self-expression, and their actual achievement in this by no means always coincides with their age in years. Nor are their physical parents the only members of society who can stand in this matter *in loco parentis* towards them. It may be that in one case a man is right to condition his neighbour after the manner of the behaviourist, because that is at the moment the manner of help he needs, while in another case to do so would be to do gross violence to his growing manhood. In particular, any man whose duty it is to exercise leadership among his fellows—be it pastoral, political, industrial or of any other kind—must continually be having to face the question of what kind of influence the occasion demands.

These problems, provided by the fifth of our fundamental tenets, are further complicated by contributions from the third and fourth. The ideal is that the right thing should be done freely. In this particular case, is it better that the right thing should be done, no matter how, or that a certain individual's freedom should be given its chance, at no matter what cost to society ? And from the point of view of that individual's own development, is practice in the habit of doing what is right, or in the habit of asserting his freedom, the more needed at this point in his career? If in this case there has to be deficiency on one side or the other, on which side shall it be? These two " poles " in the constitution of the perfect freedom to which we aspire provide for us on our journey a standing tension. It is the condition of our continuing to travel that we resolve the tension in one case only to be faced by the necessity of a fresh act of resolution in the next.

I do not see that there is any way of laying down any rule of thumb by which such problems can be solved in advance. If the passing of time presents us with situations as the plastic raw material for our creative activity, there is no escape from the conclusion that life is an art, and demands the artist's intuition of all who would live aright.[1] The most that can be said is that if we are convinced of the main thesis of this essay and the last—that the purpose of creation is the eliciting of perfect human freedom—then we must never be false to this aim, never allow the easier method of conditioning behaviour to be a *substitute* for the more difficult method of winning free response. Where either is equally possible, the latter must be chosen. The former is only justifiable in order to clear away obstacles in the way of the latter, or to restore the balance of a one-sided development. Skilful staging of the externals of public worship is justifiable as a means to set free the spirit of man for fuller self-devotion to God. It is probable that in the more darkly Satanic districts of our modern industrial towns a greater degree of conditioning is needed than in that little Cornish church where an endowed benefaction secures that clear glass in the window by the departed donor's seat shall always give his successor in that pew an unobstructed vision of the countryside.

These problems press with special force, as has been said, on those who are called to leadership. They have to face continual temptation to run other people's lives for them. Some of us err by under-exercising our power to condition

---

[1] I have tried to develop this point in the next essay and in *And Was Made Man*, chap. ii.

our fellows, cloaking our cowardice under the guise of an exaggerated respect for their freedom. Others err by trampling underfoot the demands of that freedom, content if they succeed in regimenting their fellows into marching along the straight and narrow way. And it is not only those who in a special sense are leaders that have to find their way through this problem. All men are social animals, and there is no one of us who can for ever avoid facing the question " Am I my brother's keeper ? "

The responsibility is great. But if there is any meaning in the ancient words which speak of man being made in God's image, it is that man is given by God a co-operative share in His creative activity, and he must rise up to this responsibility if he is to become himself. This leads us to the thought that in God's relationship to us there must be still much of the external conditioning as well as of the control through " grace." We cannot trace the finger of God *only* in those influences which we receive through our conscious personal communion with Him. He is moulding and shaping us in all our behaviouristic development before we ever become aware of what is going on. And still we may need more of such conditioning than we can know. But we may be sure that neither in the past, nor in the present, nor in the future can that conditioning be thought of as constricting our true growth in freedom. In so far as it is due to His direct willing it is developing in us the nature of finite beings capable of freedom ; in so far as our freedom is constricted by external conditioning it is due to the misuse of their creative power by our fellow-creatures, and here the omnipotence of God is made ours through grace to transform even such con-striction into the means of its own defeat.

If this be true, then there is no more mistaken approach to the problem of the miraculous than that which regards God as reserving to Himself a right to interfere in human life which he has renounced in respect of the " laws " of the physical world. It would appear more reasonable to regard the physical order as the passive instrument of God's will aiming at the creation of free beings. It can be controlled as they can not, and there would be no irrationality in accepting adequate evidence that it had sometimes deviated from its commonly observed uniform manner of behaviour, if that deviation could be thought of as fulfilling the aim of the whole process—the eliciting of perfect finite freedom. It is not without significance that He whom we believe to have been God incarnate thought of the power over storms and bread and mountains as lying in His hands, but of men as those into whose hands He was to give the power over Himself.

# VI. COMPROMISE, TENSION AND PERSONALITY

## I

It is sometimes said that the idea of personality is the master key with which to solve the problems of the universe. It may be so; but when the nature of the key turns out itself to be one of the most baffling of the problems, its use as an instrument is not so simple after all. Indeed the word "personality" is one of those slippery words of which one has to be perennially cautious, one of those words which mean one thing at one time and another at another, one thing to this man and another to that. Perhaps it is just because of this that it often seems to provide us with so satisfying a solution of profound mysteries, for it buries them in the depths of its own indeterminateness. It is therefore necessary for anyone who would use the word as a counter in the philosophical exchange to scrutinise it very carefully and declare openly with all possible accuracy just what it is intended to convey.

On the other hand, when a straightforward, non-philosophical Christian says that he believes in a God who is personal, there is not much doubt about what he has in mind. He distinguishes between persons and things. The former are beings like himself, capable of making up their minds to do things and then doing them, towards whom he acts as fellow human beings. The latter have no minds to make up, and move not of their own will but willy-nilly in an ordered system of cause and effect. When he speaks of God as personal he means that the source and ground of all things, and the true object of worship, is One better thought of after the analogy of a person than of a thing, after the analogy of one who knows what it is to make up his mind to do things, and to explain why he did them in terms which imply reliance on other men's capacity to understand the grounds on which he thought them worth doing.

Let us, then, take as our starting-point this one prominent element in human personality, the capacity to run our lives on the basis of deciding what is worth doing and then setting ourselves to do it. This capacity is, of course, something which we need to develop and strengthen as life goes on. It exists in very varying degrees in different cases. But to be entirely without it would be to lack one of the distinctive characteristics of human beings, who may be thought of fundamentally as growing in the extent to which they direct their lives in accordance with the conscious pursuit of what is recognised as worth while.

This leads at once to the question, What is worth while? As soon as that question is raised the study of ethics is in existence, a study which now has a long history and is not ended yet. The first and most obvious answer to give is to say Pleasure, and this answer is given both by ethics in its infancy and by each individual human infant when he first begins to run his own life. But the true beginning of the serious study of ethics comes with realisation of the inadequacy of this answer, with the apprehension of the clash between what is pleasant and what is truly worth while. At a much later stage comes the discovery that no satisfactory answer can be given in terms of self-interest of any kind whatsoever. At this point it is necessary not to be led astray by the ambiguity latent in the use of the word " satisfy." It is true that in searching for what is worth while man is searching for that which will satisfy him as an end to live for. From this it might be concluded that since he is seeking for what will satisfy him, the answer must be in terms of self-interest. But this is a merely verbal sophistication, and to learn to see one's way through it might well be called the *pons asinorum* of ethics. When we pass from words to facts we are faced with a truth which, though paradoxical in words, is a commonplace in experience. Only that will satisfy man which is not sought because it will satisfy. What he needs is a cause objectively existent and greater than himself, to which he can devote himself because, no matter what may become of him, its victory must be secured. Anyone who has ever played football knows by experience something of the truth of this, or at least has caught a glimpse of what that experience might be, could he conquer himself sufficiently to enter into it. It is in such experiences that man rises to the heights of his capacity, and becomes aware of a satisfactoriness in life and a happiness of which, perhaps, he had never dreamed. This truth speaks from every page of such writings as the letters of Edwin Austin Abbey.[1]

There is something in man, then, which will not be satisfied by anything less than an objective cause into which he can throw himself because its victory is supremely worth while. From this point of view the whole human race appears as needing this, though with very varying degrees of awareness of their need and of its nature. Some are still at the pleasure stage, others, having passed beyond that, are still pursuing their own interest in some form or other. Many others have discovered the futility of this, and are frankly puzzled what to put in its place. Is not one of the prevalent notes of life to-day that of disillusionment and a sense of having somehow missed whatever would have made life worth living ?

It is no use pretending that the problem is an easy one to solve. What is really worth while ? The Roman poet essayed an answer when he said *Exegi monumentum aere perennius*, but a few centuries later another poet had seen the hollowness of this hope and dismissed the spur of fame as " the last infirmity of noble mind." We look back over our lives, and see the alternating periods, the happy stimulating days when we had something to live for alternating with a curious sense of emptiness when the longed-for end had been achieved. At one time, perhaps, it was some examination before us which filled the horizon, at another the gaining of a place in some athletic team, at another the appointment to some position or other, at another the passing of some measure by a governmental body. In this way we learned the need of some unifying aim or purpose which should not be exhausted in any one particular achievement in time ; and even when we have discovered the need of this, there remain problems enough when we ask by what particular acts it is best to be pursued. Is it more worth while for the scholar-priest to follow the example of Browning's grammarian and

[1] See *An American Soldier* (Houghton Mifflin).

rigidly to limit himself to the pursuit of his own main line of study in the hope that by so doing he may eventually some day make some contribution to human knowledge, or to turn aside to preach sermons and write ephemeral papers, or to be at the disposal of anyone who may come in to consult him at any hour of the day or night? Moreover, what of the multitudes who are never conceited enough to raise any such questions concerning themselves, but are contented to live and die like the subject of Gray's "Elegy"? And, still further, what of those who have given their lives in whole-hearted devotion to some cause which ends in failure, who in their old age live to see all that they had toiled for tumble to pieces and be laid in the dust? How can we find some conception of what is worth while in life which is adequate to act as a unifying principle for all lives at all times under all conditions?

It is clear that the cause for which we are to live and die must be one which both transcends the order of time and space and is yet capable of embodiment in particular temporo-spatial acts. It must transcend them each and all because we need it to give them, each and all, the quality of being worth while. It is the pursuit of a "worth-whileness" entirely within time and space which crowns achievement not with satisfaction but with "slump." Yet it must not be such that it is indifferent to the particular acts in and through which it is served by man; it evacuates life of all meaning to treat the particular events of which it is made up as extrinsic means to an end in no way immanent in themselves.

The Christian view of the purpose of life as the embodiment on earth of the transcendent realities of beauty, truth and goodness makes its appeal just because of this fundamental fact of man's nature, his need of a cause which can be served in and through the events of his earthly life, but so that in each achievement he achieves something not wholly comprised in the particular act but for eternity. In order to understand the significance of this view it is necessary to reflect upon what happens in detail in any attempt to carry it into practice.

## II

From our point of view as living within the time series the true life of man would seem to be essentially creative. Whether it would so appear *sub specie aeternitatis* is a question which for the present we may well leave on one side. The important thing is to recognise that in the course of the history of our lives in time novelties do occur which, so far as the time series is concerned, are truly new, and which we have a hand in creating. Moreover these novelties, while created out of and embodied in the things of earth, are valuable just in so far as they embody what is transcendently worth while. Out of the block of marble comes the statue and is embodied in it ; out of the scraping of string on string comes the music, embodied in the vibrations that contact sends forth. As we listen to it, are we seeking for an escape from the world of reality in an unreal world of phantasy, or are we lifted up for a while into that truly real world for which we are made, for want of whose life we are restless until we find rest in it ? It is the affirmation of our faith that in this experience in time of communion with the beauty embodied in the things of time we catch a glimpse of the celestial world of timeless reality.

But it is not only through artistic creation that man creates on earth embodiments of eternity. There are other elements in the heavenly world which can on this earth be embodied in events of time and space, such as justice, freedom, brother-hood, and love. Out of the circumstances of our earthly life we may create the earthly embodiments of these heavenly realities, using danger as the raw material of courage, suspense as that of perseverance, disappointment of patience, success of gratitude and humility. Business contacts are the stuff out of which brotherhood and honesty are to be created, and politics provide the medium for the creator of social justice. So the list might be indefinitely extended. Of course, like the artist, we need our technique, we need to know and respect the " laws " in accordance with which our raw material can be worked. The well-meaning fool may be almost as great a danger as the clever knave, and idealistic aims must never be *substituted* for the diligent pursuit of such disciplines as history, psychology, economics and other sciences. But, in order that we may not lose the full fruit of these studies, we must never forget that the call to creative activity, to the creation of earthly embodiments of heavenly realities, is the true secret of human life. The extent to which each action exhibits the quality of novelty varies. Actions differ in scale in degrees of novelty, to which corresponds a scale of degrees of creative intensity. It is true that every human action is a unique event, and no human action is devoid of the quality of novelty. Still a great proportion of our lives is occupied in more or less routine activities, or in meeting certain standard situations in which there is no question as to the right creative response. We follow precedent and reproduce anew what has been done before. But this must not blind us to the fact that with the passing of time fresh circumstances are continually arising, and at any moment there may come into the present from the womb of the future an unprecedented situation which calls for an unprecedented creative act, in which the element of novelty is at its highest and the creative self-expression most intense. In the more straightforward normal stretches of life we must keep alive our sense of the novelty and creativeness of human action, keeping ourselves in training for the great moment when it comes, lest coming suddenly it find us sleeping. " Watch therefore, for ye know not the day nor the hour."

To explain life in terms of what is worth while is to give an account of how out of earthly circumstances can be created in space and time embodiments of heavenly realities.

### III

When we ask what are the conditions most conducive to the exercise of this creative activity we are faced by the fact that they are conditions of conflict or tension. It is the unsolved puzzle, the unreconciled contradiction, which calls forth our creative response. We can see it at work in the crossword fiend who will get out his pencil and paper if given an inch of elbow-room in a crowded subway train, or in the golf maniac who is never so happy as when coaxing a little white ball into a hole from which he promptly removes it. Is there any joy more characteristically human than the joy of meeting problems which elicit our creative activity in devising their solutions ? I well remember the enthusiasm with which a certain mechanic whom I once met talked of his work. He was in the repair department of a large factory, and his duty was to go when summoned and deal with any break-downs in machinery that might have occurred. What gave the work its fascination was that he was continually being called upon to deal with machines that he had never seen before. It was " up to " him from his general knowledge of machinery to discover and put right the cause of failure, and in the continual challenge of new problems calling for new solutions he found his joy in his work.

From this point of view it is remarkable how fertile is this world we live in in providing ethical problems rather than solutions. Is it not, indeed, characteristic of our experience that we are continually being called upon to face apparent antinomies which persist from generation to generation, ever calling anew to be solved *ambulando* and remaining to provide new problems for successive ages ? We have only to think of the rival claims of the world-affirming and the world-denying elements in religion, of the tension between religion and morality, of the demands of authority and freedom, of the conflicting loyalties to Church and State, of the necessity to Christianity of both its Catholic and its Protestant " moments," or of that profoundly illuminating reflection of Baron von Hügel that " Jesus cures pain and disease as though they could not be utilised, whilst Jesus also trains and empowers souls to utilise their sufferings as though they were incurable."

Now what may perhaps be called a static or mechanistic logic is impatient of all such antinomies, and demands an immediate " either or " solution of them. But such a logic is inadequate for human life at its best. What is needed is a dynamic or personal logic, for which one element in being a " person " is to be, as it were, a focal point where various claims come together and require on our part the creative act of imposing upon them a solution which is worth while. This creative activity is most intense, and human life rises to its greatest heights, in cases where no following of precedent or application of predetermined rule can tell us what to do—

where we have to launch out into the deep and boldly invent a solution in which the quality of novelty is at its highest degree, as when Dr. Cram, faced by the problem of covering with a Gothic tower a space larger than ever before presented to the designer of such a building, created that new thing in Gothic architecture, the glorious tower which we hope to see crowning the Cathedral of St. John the Divine in New York.

In his interesting and valuable treatment of the ethics of compromise [1] Dr. Kirk approaches this view of the matter, but he does not seem to me to recognise sufficiently clearly the intrinsic importance of tension in the structure of things as the necessary ground of our highest human activity.    It is surely necessary to distinguish between compromise which is a refusal to choose where choice ought to be made, and maintenance of tension as the condition of a series of creative acts. It is just because this pain must be cured and that endured, because on this occasion we must support Church against State and on that support State against Church, because here we must defer to authority and there assert our freedom, and because until the particular circumstances have arisen it is impossible to lay down in advance what the right action will be, that life is such as to offer to us continually fresh opportunities for the exercise of our highest human creative activity.

I have suggested that whatever else may be included in the conception of human personality, one highly significant element in the being of a human person is to be one who, when faced by the tension of conflicting demands, neither of which can be in principle denied *in toto*, is called upon to exercise creative activity in the devising of actions that are worth while as embodiments on earth of heavenly realities.    If, then, we are to think of God as in any way " personal," this will surely imply, at least, that we think of Him in His relations with us as sharing in these interests, and as Himself acting on grounds of what is " worth while," rather than by analogy from the impersonal laws of nature or " static logic."    It is in this way that our religion has always thought of God.    We see this in the Living God of the Old Testament and the God who is

---

[1] See *Conscience and its Problems* (Longmans, Green & Co., 1927), pp. 362–368.

Love of the New, and it is significant that two recent writers reaffirm the demand for a conception of God which shall carry on this tradition.  Thus in " Reality " Canon Streeter writes : " Just so far as it seems to be a necessity for thought to conceive the Power behind phenomena as concretely personal, I submit that the anthropomorphism of Jesus is intellectually in advance of the rationalised abstractions of a Hegel, a Haeckel or a Herbert Spencer," and Dr. Rawlinson makes a similar affirmation of belief at the end of his Bampton Lectures. I suggest that a corroborative line of argument in support of this position may be based on our recognition of these antinomies or tensions as permanent elements embodied in the structure of the world in which as creative beings we find ourselves called upon to live.  A static logic may find in them obstacles to the rationality of the universe, but a deeper insight can see in them evidence that what the Author and Source of all being cares about is our exercise of our highest activities, and that He has so devised the circumstances of our life as to elicit from us the response for which He looks.

# VII. BIRTH CONTROL AND CHRISTIAN ETHICS

## I

THE Christian moralist of to-day is bound to face the question of birth control, and it is not easy to give an immediate answer to the question: " What is the teaching of Christianity on the subject ? " In spite of the asseverations of certain religious preachers and journalists who, whenever it is mentioned, refuse to admit that for Christians the matter can be anything but *chose jugée*, the plain man continues in doubt. Very often he would be glad of some clear guidance, of some voice commanding his respect which would say " This is the way, walk ye in it." But that voice is hard to hear. So far as the Church of England is concerned, the nearest approach to authoritative guidance that has been made is contained in a memorandum issued by a large majority of the bishops in 1914, which was drawn up to help the clergy in advising their flocks on this subject. This document, admirable in its temper of pastoral care and Christian wisdom, seems nevertheless to have faded into obscurity, and is seldom referred to when birth control is discussed at the present time.[1] Moreover, much has happened since the beginning of 1914, and the plain man is apt to wonder whether the bishops then wrote with a full appreciation of all the factors of the problem as they can be seen in the light of present-day knowledge and experience, and he wonders the more when he finds that in a book of 1923, no less admirable in its temper of pastoral care and Christian wisdom than the bishops' memorandum, another view is taken.[2] In view of such facts, he feels that it is of no use to proclaim that the matter has been

---

[1] It is printed in full on pp. 382–388 of *The Declining Birth Rate* (Chapman & Hall, 1917).
[2] See *Men, Women and God*, by A. H. Gray (S.C.M.).

settled long ago once and for all by the voice of the Church. If the teaching of the Anglican bishops in 1914, which was the traditional teaching of the Church, is to be commended to-day, it must be not merely because of its agreement with the traditional teaching of the Church, but because it approves itself to consciences unafraid to welcome the light of the knowledge of truth from whatever corner it may shine.

This demand that the question, as it is put in secular circles to-day, should be openly faced by religious leaders, is a right demand. The practical problems of morality always have reference to the particular circumstances in which men and women find themselves. It is always possible, as the history of the world goes on, for elements of novelty to arise in the circumstances in which we have to live our lives, and the demand that moral guidance should take account of these elements of novelty is always a right demand. The classical instance is the work of the great Jesuit moralists of the seventeenth century, who faced the problems of the modern as contrasted with the mediaeval world. We are gradually learning that a conception of our duty to our neighbour adequate for feudalism is inadequate to modern industrial civilisation. Are there, then, at the present time elements of novelty which necessitate a reconsideration of the question of birth control?

There may justly be said to be three facts which have emerged into prominence of recent years, which ought to be considered, about which men doubt whether they have been sufficiently taken into account in the past.

In the first place, there is the political problem of population. Sometimes this is put forward by eugenists as the problem of the excessive multiplication of undesirable elements in society : sometimes as a purely economic problem, with reference merely to the quantity and not to the quality of the population of a country. It is said that the nineteenth century was, on the whole, a century of increasing material wealth and increasing capacity to support human life on the earth, that the limits of expansion have been reached, and that the problem now is how to cut our coat according to our cloth. Again, from another point of view, the growing demand that the State should guarantee maintenance for all its members is held to carry with it a right on the part of the State to prescribe the number of members for whose sustenance it will undertake responsibility.

Secondly, it may be said that the woman's point of view has comparatively recently found open expression for the first time. The last half-century has witnessed a remarkable growth in the higher education of women, and with this has come a revelation of the sufferings of women in over-frequent bearing of children through the thoughtlessness of men, a revolt against the treatment of women as merely child-bearing machines, and a demand on the part of women to be recognised as having intellectual and aesthetic, as well as physical, contributions to make to the good of mankind.

Thirdly, there are the investigations of psychologists, which have a great influence on the thought of the present day. It is probably the fear of repressed complexes, or neuroses, or whatever other terms may be used for the psychological bogies, which more than anything else drives men and women to-day to the use of artificial methods to avoid the conception of children. It is probably the thought that the traditional Christian teaching ignores these very real dangers that leads to its being widely questioned at the present time.

## II

It is already clear that the subject divides itself into two parts. There is first the question whether it is justifiable at all for a husband and wife to attempt to control the number of children which they are to bring into the world, and secondly, if this be answered in the affirmative, there arises the question of the methods to be adopted to achieve that end. Of the arguments we have been considering, the political and the feminist arguments relate to the former of these questions, the psychological more directly to the latter.

Now on the first question, it must surely be generally agreed that birth control of some sort or other is not merely permissible : it is often a positive duty. In this essay I am not concerned with the relation between the State and its members, important as are the issues raised by that relation

for Christian ethics. I shall therefore leave entirely un-
touched the question whether the State would be justified
in prescribing the maximum number of children to be produced by any particular marriage. I wish rather to consider
the advice that should be given by a Christian minister to
any of his flock who should consult him on these matters.
Here, the political argument appears as viewed from the side
of the individual who realises his responsibility as a member
of the State, and who realises that his obligations as a Christian
include his doing his duty as a citizen.

It is sometimes argued by rash controversialists, to whom
the very term " birth control " is anathema, that the only
motives which could ever lead to a man's desiring to limit
the size of his family were selfish and unworthy. Very
little reflection suffices to show that this is simply not true.
A man may honestly be conscious of vocation to work which
he can perform efficiently if his family be small, but in
which he will be severely hampered by financial embarrass-
ment if it be large. Or a man may be honestly convinced
that his duty to the State forbids him to bring into existence
a number of human beings for whose maintenance he cannot
make himself responsible, and who will therefore become a
burden on the community. Again, a man may know that
to subject his wife to the frequent bearing of children will
be unjustifiable and unchristian cruelty. So far from ignoring
these facts, the Christian teacher may often have to call
attention to them, and to help members of his flock to see
that the path of duty may lie along the line of birth control.

So far nothing has been said which is not in agreement
with the traditional teaching of the Church. But now the
more difficult question must be faced of the methods of
birth control. Here there is a vital divergence between the
traditional teaching, as set forth, for instance, in the memorandum of the Anglican bishops, and the propaganda of many
present-day teachers. The former recognise as justifiable no
methods other than the voluntary abstinence from intercourse on the part of husband and wife for more or less
prolonged periods ; the latter advocate the use of physical
devices which will make that intercourse possible while
removing the possibility of ensuing childbirth.

It is here that the psychological bogies terrify men and women into agreement with the latter view. Not that psychologists are all agreed. There are those who maintain that the divorce of sexual indulgence from any idea of its natural issue is itself productive of neuroses. But nevertheless the prevalent opinion among men and women at the present day is that self-denial in the sphere of sex is the main source of those repressed complexes which are the chief among human ills, and that the traditional Christian teaching is heartlessly indifferent to the crop of mental disorders which will inevitably spring up in any field wherein that word is sown. This issue must be faced if that teaching is to be maintained.

## III

To face the issue, the Christian must stand squarely on the firm rock of the first principles of his faith. " The chief end of man," says a famous statement of those principles, " is to glorify God and to enjoy Him for ever." Now the God of Christianity is the God revealed in growing clearness to the Jews, and in His fullness in Jesus Christ, a God whose fundamental qualities are ethical. What is involved in belief in such a God has been set forth in recent times in such works as Professor Sorley's " Moral Values and the Idea of God " and Dr. Jacks's " Religious Perplexities." Briefly, it may be said that for the Christian, goodness is the only thing worth seeking in life, for only in the achievement of goodness does the spirit of man find that freedom which is of all things most precious. The man to whom the Christian message speaks is the man who longs above all else to be able to say " I am the master of myself." To such a man this life exists as the sphere wherein this freedom is to be won. What he asks of the world is that it should give him opportunities of playing the man. Difficulties, dangers and pains will be taken as providing such opportunities, and in so far as he triumphs over them, he will count them all worth while. For the freedom which he seeks is the pearl of great price, and he would rather suffer and be free than live in ease and in bondage of soul.

Now the Christian conception of divine grace holds that it is help given by God to man which does not supplant but increases his freedom. It is not our task here to explain this conception, but simply to note the fact of its existence.[1] Christianity maintains that though man is unable by his own effort to be the master of his soul, it is offered to him by God through Christ to share in the divine omnipotence. So St. Paul says, " I can do all things through Christ which strengtheneth me." The service of God is perfect freedom.

We come back to the problem of birth control. Let us imagine a man and his wife honestly convinced that it is their duty to limit the size of their family. They fear that they are perhaps on the horns of a dilemma. Either they must bring into the world children whose advent they cannot justify, or they must themselves reap a crop of psychological disturbances through repressing their natural instincts. Two ways of escape are offered to them—the one the way of physical aids to avoid childbirth, the other the way of reliance on divine grace in the exercise of self-control. The whole question, when so put, surely resolves itself into that of the comparative value set upon freedom from strain on the one hand, and on self-control on the other. The man or woman who values self-control for itself as an intrinsic element in that freedom of spirit which is the goal of life, will not hesitate in the choice. If there is a help which does not diminish but increases their freedom, it is to that help that they will turn.

There are, then, two things which the defender of the traditional teaching of the Church on birth control can say about the fear of psychological bogies. In the first place, he can point out that these bogies arise and have power where life is lived with its chief emphasis on the negation of desire. But such a life is lived, so to speak, backwards : the liver of it keeps his eyes fixed with reluctant longing on the things he is doing without, and slowly and stumblingly walks backward away from them. But this is not the life commended by the Christian. The life he stands for is positive, not negative. The liver of it has turned round and is facing

[1] But see Essays IV and V above.

G

upwards towards the self-control and the freedom for which above all he passionately cares, and in the heat of that passion are burnt up those lesser fires from which otherwise the psychological bogies might be gendered.

But secondly, and chiefly, he will speak of the divine grace. The psychological bogies fatten upon fear; against the confidence which comes of faith in God and the power of His grace they have no might. I have suggested in an earlier essay that " repressed complexes " hold much the same place in the thought of to-day that was given to evil spirits by the early Christians.[1] As faith in Christ then set men and women free from the tyranny of demons, so now the Christian message is that in the power of Christ the Christian can laugh at the bogies of the morbid psychologist. It is ludicrous indeed to think that one who shares in the victory of the Resurrection cannot control his own passions, and when once the absurdity of that suggestion strikes us, the fear and the danger it breeds are gone. He who laughs wins, and those who are justified by faith have boldness to laugh.

It is surely the obscuring of this fact that the essence of the Christian message is the offer of power that leads to our doubts about the true Christian teaching on birth control. It is commonly assumed that the Christian teacher exists to perform the absurd function of demanding of men and women that they should perform duties which are beyond their strength. But this is to make Christianity a religion of Law, not of Gospel. The Christian teacher does indeed recognise the inability of men and women to do what they ought, but the essence of his message is the proclamation that Christ offers the power to enable them to rise in response to His call. It is that message of help which the man who cares only for self-control and freedom will hear, the message which inspires both words and music in the well-known anthem of Haydn :

> " Insanae et Vanae Curae
> Invadunt mentes nostrae
> Saepe furore replent
> Corda privata spe.

[1] See Essay II, above.

Quid prodest, O Mortalis,
Conari pro mundanis,
Si coelos negligas ?
Sunt fausta tibi cuncta,
Si Deus est pro te."

The traditional teaching of the Church on the subject of
birth control sometimes sounds out of date.   But to those
who take a long view, it is the teaching which has the future
in its keeping.   Let us suppose that its message goes un-
heeded, and that, in a widespread revolt from all that seems
old-fashioned, men and women generally solve their problem
by the use of physical means to avoid childbirth.   Sooner
or later there will surely come a great weariness of bondage
to the passions of the flesh : the spirit of man will not be for
ever content to meet its difficulties by avoiding them, it will
long to assert itself, crying out that it *will* be free.   Where
then will be the Church of Christ ?   Will she have forfeited
her right to answer with the message of hope those who cry
out for freedom ?   Or will she then be able to save men and
women from the danger of a Puritan reaction to exaggerated
asceticism by having proclaimed consistently her Gospel of
grace ?

Without some such message of hope, it is hard to see a
future which shall not find men and women passing alternately
through ages of self-indulgence and of unreasoning self-
denial.   The question is worth considering whether this or
acceptance of the Christian life is likely to produce the larger
crop of psychological ills.


## IV

It remains to face certain practical questions that arise
from the position that has been taken up.   We began by
asking what counsel the Christian minister should be prepared to give his flock on the subject of birth control.   So
far, what we seem to have done is to have suggested that
to the man or woman seeking his help he should give a sketch
of the ideal Christian life, and show that there the problem is
solved.   But our difficulties arise just because we do not live
ideal Christian lives, and the men and women in need of

priestly counsel and advice often need it just because they have not the faith which leads to saving laughter.

In his book, "Some Principles of Moral Theology," Mr. Kirk has called attention to the difference of the spirit pervading different systems of moral theology according as they are based on the consideration of the legal minimum necessary to salvation, or of the virtues as the ideal of character. Perhaps an analogy may be taken from the curricula of a university. In a university we have honours schools and pass schools, and any teacher knows the difference of spirit evoked by following these different courses. The pass man asks "What must I do to get through?" but that question never even crosses the mind of the true honours man. The question for him is how most thoroughly to master the subject of his study. To the academic mind the problem before us takes the form of the question: "Is life an honours school or a pass school?"

That life is an honours school, in which the question to be asked is not "What must I do to be saved?" but "What may I do, being redeemed?" is surely the only possible answer for the Christian teacher. "Be ye perfect," said Christ, "even as your Father in heaven is perfect." But nevertheless, the Christian priest, like the university tutor, has to deal with pass men as well as honours men. A university, of its charity, provides a course of education suitable to their capacity. Can the Church allow a pass course of life, differing from the honours course set before those to whom she says "Be ye perfect"?

It is interesting to notice how, when we begin discussing such a subject as birth control, we find ourselves involved in discussing the classical questions at issue in the history of Christian thought. Belief in the necessity of divine grace, so strongly asserted by St. Augustine as against Pelagius, has been seen to be a presupposition of the Christian solution of the problem of birth control in general. And now, when we approach the problem of the individual application of that general teaching, we raise the question which perhaps most vitally separates the Catholic from the Protestant mind. In all its protesting, Protestantism has always protested most vigorously against any recognition of a distinction between the highest life and the permissible life, between what we have ventured to call the life of the honours man and the life of the pass man, whereas that distinction in one form or another is a commonplace in Catholic moral theology.

It is sometimes said of Catholics that on moral questions " you always know where you are with them. They have rigid rules and make no exceptions." If this were true it would be a very grave charge, and the Catholic apologist would be hard put to it to defend his system as adequate to the multifarious needs of men and women. But the truth is that the great strength of the Catholic system is the machinery it has devised for dealing with exceptions. This has an important bearing on our present discussion. We are considering how to avoid producing psychological ills through the enjoining of commandments harder than men can bear. The danger is that of producing in men and women a chronic sense that they are objects of displeasure to God through failing to carry out what they believe to be His will. Historically, the Catholic method of meeting this difficulty has been twofold. First, there has been the distinction between those who are and those who are not called to follow " counsels of perfection " ; and secondly, for those who fail to live up to the level demanded of them, there has been the provision of the priest commissioned to say " Go in peace. The Lord hath put away thy sin." When Protestantism revolted against these methods, there arose at once an urgent need of some substitute to preserve the sanity of sinful man. This need was met by the emergence of the Protestant doctrine of assurance. The Catholic who kneels to listen to the priestly word of absolution and the Protestant who relies on his election by God have in common that in their religion which is of chief moment. For both, their salvation depends not on what they have themselves achieved, but is accepted as a free gift of God sealed to them through the blood of Jesus Christ.

It is a curious fact that at the present time Protestants are more ready than Catholics to admit the justifiability of the use of physical methods of birth control. Viewed *a priori*, one might have expected the Catholic system, with its recognition of different levels of vocation, to have been more easily able to find room for such a position as is adopted by Dr. A. H. Gray, whilst any such accommodation to human weakness might have been thought impossible for the Protestant mind, which demands of all men that they should aim at the highest. But here it is Protestantism rather than Catholicism which shows a tendency to make the pass course the standard. That this is so may perhaps be explained as follows. The provision of a system of individual absolution makes it possible for Catholicism to maintain the higher level as the only one explicitly recognised, while dealing definitely as exceptions with all failures to attain to it. Those who repudiate such methods of dealing with the problem have to include in their statement of the rule considerations which those who do not live at the strictest level may apply to their own cases.

## V

It is time to try to summarise the preceding argument, and to state as definitely as possible the conclusions that may be arrived at. Enough has been said to show that the question of birth control provides problems which demand open-minded consideration by Christian moralists, and that Christian ministers are justified when they ask that the leaders of different Christian bodies should provide them with some authoritative guidance which shall win respect by being clearly based on a frank recognition of the difficulties of the points at issue. In the meantime, and as a suggestion towards the formation of such considered judgments, I would venture to propose the following conclusions :

First, in open teaching and preaching, the Church must adopt as the only possible view of the Christian life what I have called the " honours school " attitude. It must be steadily maintained that the one and only purpose of life in the flesh is the winning of goodness through the exercise of freedom. Men and women must be urged to realise that self-control and spiritual freedom are things intrinsically worth seeking for their own sakes. They must be encouraged to adopt a positive attitude towards these things of supreme value, so that self-denial becomes not a paralysing matter of mere negation, but an element in the quest of their hearts' desire.

Secondly, the Church should lay the greatest stress on the Gospel of divine grace as the offer of power to be free. Men and women must be taught that by faith in the power of God offered to them through Christ they can laugh at the psychological bogies, and be set free from them.

But thirdly, the Christian priest must be prepared in his individual dealings to help those who are unable to laugh, and those who, after honest and fair consideration, believe themselves justified in making use of physical means to avoid childbirth. In such cases they should urge the consideration that by so doing they run the risk of losing the highest things in life, and should encourage them to make trial of the power of God and put their faith to the test of relying on God's grace to set them free. But throughout they must labour to save their flock from reaping the fruits of psychological ills through falling into a chronic state of thinking of themselves as objects of God's displeasure. When a man believes that in adopting other methods of birth control than self-control he is doing that which is displeasing to God, then he should be taught to seek the remedy for sin in the forgiveness of God which depends not on his own achievements but on the work of Christ. When, in spite of all the considerations that have been urged, men and women honestly believe themselves to be justified in the sight of God in using physical methods of birth control, their consciences must be respected, and they must be assured that so long as they do what they believe to be right they do what is pleasing to God and may continue to share freely in the communion of the Church. If they are wrong, they will come to see this not through being hardened in opposition by excommunication, but through their sharing in the life of the Church. Only the Church must continue to preach that for the Christian the standard of life he must set before himself is the highest, and to proclaim to all men the possibility of this life through the gospel of freedom and power.

Nevertheless, a certain difficulty remains. At the beginning of this essay we saw that genuine elements of novelty in the present situation make it impossible for the question of birth control to be decided by reference to past precedents alone. The upshot of these novel elements is that to-day the traditional Christian teaching on the matter requires an unprecedented degree of continence within marriage. In past ages economic standards and the accepted view of woman's vocation enabled the majority of husbands and wives to avoid facing the issue which presses so hard to-day. To-day, if prolonged abstinence is to be the method of birth control, it must be recognised as the normal state of married life, and Lord Dawson of Penn asks a very pertinent question when he writes : " Though no doubt possible with individuals, is so rigid a restraint likely to exist throughout whole classes in the community ? " [1]

To maintain unchanged the traditional Christian teaching will not be to maintain unchanged the sexual habits of Christendom. It will require nothing less than a revolution in those habits, and a man would be foolish to expect such a revolution to be accomplished in a moment. The Christian need not be afraid of having to proclaim revolutionary doctrine ; he has admirable precedent for regarding his religion as most truly itself when engaged in turning the world upside down. But the lesson of history is that while God uses His Church to effect revolutions, His method is not always catastrophic.

It is instructive to consider the development of Christian thought with regard to continence outside marriage. From the first, in the teaching and preaching of the Church, fornication was condemned, and men were expected to have no intercourse with women except within marriage. That was the ideal, and the Church never ceased to proclaim it. But it is not too much to say that the proclamation was not accompanied by a very sanguine expectation of success until the monastic movement demonstrated the possibility of chastity on a widespread scale among all sorts and conditions of men. If monasticism did nothing else, at any rate it made it possible for the Christian teacher to say with conviction to his hearers, " It is not unreasonable to expect you to be chaste."

The hypothesis is worthy of consideration that we stand to-day with regard to sexual habits within marriage where the

[1] *The Times*, September 13, 1929.

pre-monastic Church stood with regard to sexual habits out-side marriage.    If this be so, then presumably what is needed is a stage of voluntary acceptance of vows concerning marital intercourse taken by husbands and wives who recognise a vocation to pioneer activity directed towards extending the domain of human self-control over the physical processes of life.    The experimental verification, over a widespread scale, of the possibility of a new norm of married life must precede the requiring of conformity to it on the part of all sorts and conditions of men.    Those who receive and respond to this vocation will be subject to all the well-known temptations which beset " the religious life," and must above all guard against the lunacy of imagining that they are superior persons whose way of life is " higher " than that of their brethren whom God has not called to this particular work.    Possibly the best guidance that can be given to Christian pastors to-day is to suggest that the spirit in which they should proclaim the Christian ideal of continence in marriage is the spirit of encouraging vocations rather than that of requiring con-formity.    And let them not forget that to do so will entail the obligation of fitting themselves to become sympathetic and understanding counsellors of those who have taken them at their word.

## VIII.  ORIGINAL SIN AND BAPTISM

### I

WHEN a Christian who repeats the Nicene Creed and acknowledges one baptism for the remission of sins asks himself what he means by this acknowledegment, he finds (unless he belongs to that small minority of Christians among whom the baptism of infants is unknown) that he must consider the idea of original sin.  For if that clause in the Creed bears witness to any truth, in the case of infant baptism it must involve either that the infant is already in some sense sinful, or that the ceremony in some anticipatory manner helps towards the remission of sins he will afterwards commit. At first sight, perhaps, both meanings appear equally mysterious and incredible—so much so that a man may be pardoned for wondering whether it is worth while to inquire any further into the matter.  As recently as in the time of Dr. J. B. Mozley, and perhaps even later, it seemed natural to ask what theologians meant by original sin, but that question now seems hardly adequate to express the doubt which rises most readily in the mind of an ordinary man.  He will rather ask, " Do theologians mean anything at all when they talk about original sin ?  Is it not a fiction of the theological imagination, invented to justify the continuance of an out-worn baptismal ceremony which they are not bold enough to abandon ? "  And there are theologians who will agree that the ordinary man is right, and will maintain that the belief in original sin was, after all, only a corollary of belief in the literal historical accuracy of the story of the Garden of Eden, together with a theory of inspiration which constrained one to accept unquestioned St. Paul's exposition of the relation of

Adam to his successors. There is also a strain of honesty in the spirit of the age, which leads both laymen and theologians to feel impatient with the elusive conception of things which, though not themselves sinful, are " of the nature of sin." We are tempted to say that all the intricate dialectic of concupiscence is an unnecessary confusing of the issue due to a false theory of scriptural inspiration, and that the honest man will boldly accept the freedom brought by his enlightened reading of the Bible.

But it is a superficial theology which looks upon so important a doctrine as only arising because it seemed to be implied by the Scriptures interpreted after a certain manner. The reverse is the truth ; the doctrine is prior to the Bible proof of it. Through centuries of Christian tradition, it is true, the existence of original sin was linked up with the story of the Fall, because therein men seemed to find a very satisfactory explanation of its universal sway in the human race. But that universal sway was perceived as a fact of experience which, in the eyes of those whose philosophy began in wonder, needed some such explanation as it found. The story of Adam and Eve was not the origin of the doctrine, it provided a particular explanation of it, and it is poor logic to look on the discarding of any particular explanation as necessarily involving a denial of the fact.

But if the doctrine of original sin has suffered among theologians from being thought to arise from belief in the story of Adam and Eve, it has suffered still more among laymen from a failure to appreciate the nice accuracy of traditional theological expression. We are accustomed loosely to use the word " actual " as equivalent to " real "—a use which is the source of endless confusion in many departments of thought. Consequently the ordinary man is apt to think that " actual sin " is synonymous with " real sin " ; and as he finds that in the traditional theology original sin is contrasted with actual sin, he naturally concludes that original sin is in some sense unreal, a conclusion which is confirmed by the belief that the word " origin " is simply synonymous with " beginning," so that original sin either means sin committed by Adam at the beginning of the world, or sin which a man brings with him at the beginning of his life ; and this common belief that a relation of precedence in time is the whole meaning of the word " original " is the parent of much misunderstanding of the doctrine of original sin, and impatience with it.

What then, in strict accuracy, is the meaning of the traditional contrast between original sin and actual sin ? Actual sins are, as the phrase says, acts of sin, particular sins committed by particular men at particular times in the course of history. They may, indeed, be called real sins, as having the same kind of reality as any act done in the history of the world, but in that sense only, and this, of course, is far from ascribing to them the only kind of reality there is.

But granted their reality in this sense, whence do they spring ? What is their origin ? It is clearly impossible to look upon any conscious act of a man as an isolated phenomenon in the history of the world, bearing no relation to the character of the man who did it. If I tell a lie or steal sixpence, those acts are the outward expression of lying or thieving elements in my character ; they show that to a certain extent I am a liar or a thief. They may, indeed, reveal to me the fact that I am, which I never realised before, so that I say " How could I ever have done such a thing ? " But once the thing is done there is no denying the fact : I have revealed myself to be a liar and a thief, and it is this which gives the sting to remorse.

This truth may be illustrated by analogy from almost any sphere of activity. Consider a violinist or a poet. When the poet is writing poetry, or the violinist playing, they are performing acts, poetical acts and musical acts. But their poesy and musicianship are not confined to these moments ; they can only perform these actions in virtue of the characters which are always theirs ; they are poet and musician, though the one may never write another stanza or the other touch again his instrument, and when our neighbour taps our shoulder and says " Look, there goes so-and-so," we feel a thrill of admiration, though all we see is a man of very ordinary appearance walking down the street in a bowler hat. He is not now standing on the concert platform holding us spellbound by strains of inexpressible beauty, but he is the man who does this, and so there is in him much to admire. Indeed, it is because of what he is at all times that we really admire him ;

it is because he is this at all times that he can at some times play to our delight; the music in him is the source of the music that comes from him; the "actual music" he gives us springs from the "original music" in him—that is to say, from the music in him which is its origin.

Precisely similar is the relation of actual sin to original sin; the sinfulness of our character is called "original sin" as being the origin of the acts of sin we commit which are therefore summed up as "actual sin." It is, of course, true that actions in their turn influence character, but this must not be allowed to obscure the fact that they are also, and are perhaps primarily, revelations of character, so that it was no wanton fancy of theologians to postulate a sinful element in the character of all who commit actual sins as the original of those acts. We may feel doubts about their further attempt to find for this sinful element an origin in a particular act in the Garden of Eden. If so, let us seek for a better one. The element remains as the basis of their attempt and of ours.

But how far is this element of original sin in us something which needs "remission"? Our analogy of the violinist will here carry us some way. As we found that in him there is at all times something worthy of admiration, so we have found in ourselves regarded as sinners an element deserving of a very different attitude. What it needs is not admiration, but disapproval; and when we claim from God the expression of His disapproval, we hope for that atoning expression of it whereby punishment is fused with forgiveness, and the scarlet of our sin becomes as white as snow.

It is sometimes argued, however, that this so-called sinful element in us is not something for which we are responsible; if it is to be called sinful at all, it is not our sin which makes it so; if it merits divine disapproval, it is not we who need to be forgiven. This argument usually rests upon a reference to the facts of heredity, and often professes to be an exegesis of that explanation of original sin as φρόνημα σαρκός, concupiscence, or lust of the flesh, which is given in the Ninth Article of the Church of England. We inherit, it is said, certain passions at birth; these passions, if evil passions, give us a tendency to certain sins, and lead us into them. But in so doing they are of the nature of temptation rather than of sin ; and besides, in any case, our ancestors are responsible for them, not we.

In this common form of argument two reasons are given for denying such responsibility, which we must examine separately. In the first place, it is said that this inherited element of concupiscence in us is of the nature of temptation rather than of sin. A man, for example, inherits from his parents a craving for alcohol. This craving is to him a temptation for which he is to be pitied rather than blamed. Now, so far as it goes, this is, of course, perfectly true ; but it is completely irrelevant to the point at issue. Temptation is, indeed, not sin ; in so far, therefore, as inherited passions are temptations we, no more than anyone else, desire to call them sin, whether original or of any other kind. But we deny that this is what is meant by φρόνημα σαρκός, concupiscence, or original sin, at all ; we insist on a distinction between the fact that (in the words of the Article) "man . . . is of his own nature inclined to evil," and the fact that he has in his nature temptations to evil. In our analysis of the conception of original sin we have found it to be that element in the character of a man of which his sinful acts are the expression, and as such it must be distinguished from the temptations into which he falls. What is really at stake is the existence of human freedom at all, for to identify the two must end in looking on human actions as caused by something other than the man himself, something for which he is not responsible. If a man's actions are caused by temptations over which he has no control, if they are not the expression of his character, they are not his actions at all, nor have they any moral quality. Evil acts so committed are not morally evil—they are not sins. Indeed, so far from actual sin being the only real sin, apart from the reality of original sin, and its real sinfulness, there would be no such thing as actual sin at all. For actual sin is sin committed in action, and there would be no one capable of committing it. It is adding insult to injury to hinder a man who needs it from seeking atonement on the ground that he is not really a man at all.

The second reason which is given for denying that a man is responsible for his original sin is the alleged fact that, whether it be looked on as temptation, or, as we have seen is

the true view, as some active principle in him, it is to be attri-
buted to his ancestor, and not to himself.

Now, here again, we notice that to a large extent there is
no dispute. It is in strict accordance with orthodox theory
to maintain that this original sin, whatever it be, is something
the man is born with, something that is " naturally ingendered "
of him, that is prior to any particular sinful decision of his,
that is, in fact, the source of origin of such sinful decisions
when they occur. But the orthodox theory does not proceed
in consequence to deny the man's responsibility for this
original sin. It asserts it. And there are surely very good
reasons for its doing so.

We have seen that to confuse original sin with temptation
ends in denying any real manhood at all; and the same conclusion must follow from denying a man's responsibility for
original sin, truly conceived, on the ground that it is inherited.
For what element is there in the man at all of which the same
may not be said? The nature of the self is, indeed, a deep
mystery, and no attempt can be made here to state any theory
of it, but on any theory it must somehow include as con-
stituent elements of itself whatever gifts, talents, powers,
passions, weaknesses and defects the man brings with him
when he is born into this world. It is by recognising, as he
comes to self-consciousness, that these are what go to make up
himself, and by accepting the responsibility for them, that he
can claim the title " man." These make up his manhood :
they are integral parts of himself. It is so with all gifts.
One man may have a gift for ruling men, another for teaching
children, but just because they are inborn in them, and make
them the men they are, they have the responsibility for developing their characters for the service of God and man. If they
accept responsibility for one gift, and on the strength of that
acceptance claim the right to be allowed to develop it, they
must accept the responsibility for the others. If Socrates by
virtue of certain powers can claim maintenance by the State in
order that he may exercise his functions of criticism, he must
also accept the responsibility for the other less worthy elements
of his nature—for that original sin which is ingendered
of him. If, then, we may use the phrase, " The sin of Adam,"
simply as a traditional name for original sin as we have defined

it above, we see that it is no paradox, but simple truth, to maintain that " unless all men are responsible for the sin of Adam, there is no such thing as moral responsibility at all."

Let us imagine a man in whom there are certain qualities enabling him to produce music of beauty, and also certain other qualities enabling him to commit sinful acts. If he is a man worthy of the name he will say " I am by nature musical, therefore I am responsible for giving that musicianship within me what training and exercise it needs ; I am also by nature sinful, therefore I am responsible for giving that sinfulness of mine what treatment it requires." But that is to say he is responsible for having this sinfulness blotted out, or washed away from out his character, for this is the treatment sinfulness requires. He will thus naturally pass to the language of penitence—" Make me a clean heart, O God, and renew a right spirit within me," " Wash me throughly from my wickedness, and cleanse me from my sin ; for I acknowledge my faults, and my sin is ever before me." He will see nothing incongruous in praying for the remission of his original sin.

We must now pass to the second part of our inquiry, and ask whether we may reasonably believe that Baptism can avail for the remission of that sin.

## II

Our argument has proceeded so far on the line that a man must accept responsibility for what he accepts from his ancestors, because that is what he is. He is more than that, for as possessed of self-consciousness and the power of will, he lives, not in a series of actions mechanically determined by his inherited character, but by controlling and directing it. That character, however, is, so to speak, the stuff of which he is made, a fact to which we bear witness by the common use of language when we speak of a man having or lacking self-control ; it is himself that he controls. But here we must remember that there go to the making of this self which he controls, other elements besides those which he inherits, elements which are commonly summed up as coming from his environment. This contrast of environment and heredity which is found in ordinary language is generally well under-

stood, and sufficiently accurate for our present purpose.   We
need not, for example, discuss whether or no it would be more
scientific not to contrast heredity with environment, but to
look on it as pre-natal environment.   All we need to do is to
recognise the fact that a man comes into being, and is, by
drawing upon and being built up of elements not provided by
himself.   In this way he comes to birth, in this way when born
he continues to grow both physically and spiritually.   Body
and mind grow to be what they are according to what they
feed upon.   The mind of the mathematician comes from the
study of mathematics, and no amount of attention to scientific
experiments in the laboratory will produce a knowledge of
Latin and Greek.   Yet for the mathematician and the classical
scholar, these powers are of their essential being ;   they are,
indeed, the distinctive element of their individual existence,
so that in answer to the question " What is he ? " we say
" He is a mathematician," or " He is a great classic."

Here again, as in the case of hereditary factors, when considering a man's relation to his environment in this life, we
must beware of losing sight of the man himself, and of assuming that his environment fashions him willy-nilly, leaving
him no power of control over that fashioning, and so no
responsibility for what he becomes.   That we are responsible
for the " given " elements of our being is a fact of our ordinary
existence, a fact which no religion can afford to neglect, and
which is recognised by Christ, who teaches men to pray that
they be not led into temptation and for deliverance from evil ;
who knows the danger that a man may cause one of His little
ones to stumble, but who teaches, nevertheless, that it is not
what goes into a man that defiles a man but that which comes
forth from him.   If it is important that our realisation that a
man depends for his being upon the factors supplied by heredity
and environment should not blind us to the fact that he is
responsible for what he becomes, it is equally important that
our insistence on his responsibility should not close our eyes
to his need of a suitable environment if he is to grow to " the
measure of the stature of the fulness of Christ."

The records of saintly lives would seem to make it difficult
to maintain that any earthly circumstances can make such life
impossible, or to define what environment is most suitable for

the production of Christian virtue.   But if we look closer, we find surely that in all cases the constant element in the saints' environment is God Himself.   The means of God's self-revelation to His saints may differ : it may be that a man is living amid beautiful scenery in a holy community ; it may be that, in contrast to the squalor of his outward surroundings, by prayer and communion his life is hid with Christ in God. In one way or another God is with him, and it is on that divine communion that his spirit feeds.

Let us now return to our man who has come into being by inheriting certain characteristics from his ancestors, for which he accepts responsibility.   Among them are potentialities for good which need developing, and potentialities for evil which need to be removed.   Whence is he to find the means whereby to develop the one and remove the other ?   It is clear that he must draw upon what we have agreed to call his environment, and it is of vital importance to him that he shall find there the help he needs.

Now it is this which, among other things, baptism is meant to guarantee.   From the beginning it has been the ceremony of initiation by which a man becomes a member of the Church, and this aspect of it is strongly emphasised in the Baptism Service of the Church of England.   Whenever possible the service is only to be conducted by an ordained representative of the whole Church, and a minimum of three responsible members of the Church must be present to witness the ceremony.   It is a solemn action, whereby the Church guarantees to the candidate for baptism life in an environment which shall speak to him of Christ and, by offering no opportunity of exercise to the evil within him, shall effectually free him from his original sin.

We must all of us know at least some few men who are themselves, by the grace of God, effectual means of destroying evil within us.   Their influence is such that in their presence our evil passions cannot raise their heads, but creep away to hide them from the light of goodness.   In this occasional experience we have a taste of what ideally should be our life in the society of Christ's Church ; it should be an environment in which our evil passions wither away and die, because they find no encouragement to grow, or rather no opportunity at all of

growing.    By our incorporation into this community we are
set free from the bonds of the sin we inherit.    In and through
the Baptism Service the Church declares its power to negate
the evil elements in us, and the actual form of the ceremony
symbolises this washing away of the original sin.

We have so far been dealing explicitly only with the
baptism of adults, but when we turn to consider the baptism
of infants we can approach it along the same lines.    In the
case of the adult we were dealing with a man who had already
assumed responsibility for his own life, and his own willing
acceptance of the power of the Church's influence is an
essential requisite for its working.    The infant, however, is
as yet not come to self-consciousness, nor possessed of the
power of self-determination which shall be his.    Yet there
are already within him certain inherited elements of character
which will grow and develop, and for which before many
years are passed he will have to assume responsibility.    During
these years of childhood he will be drawing fresh elements
from his environment, and the question of the nature of these
elements is all-important.    Is he to find, when he comes to
know himself, the evil within him raging unchecked and
holding him in bitter servitude ?    Or shall he find that from
times long before he can remember there were going to his
making influences which choked his evil passions at the root,
and enable him now to rejoice with a pure joy at the self to
whose direction he succeeds ?    A very little reflection on the
power of the influence of surroundings on young children
is enough to make us recognise that when the godparents
promise and vow the three things in the name of the child
they are uttering no empty formula of superstitious origin and
of no value ; they have it in their hands, as representatives of
the Church, to ensure that when the child comes to know himself he shall find himself to be one who is set free from the
service of the world, the flesh and the devil, and who naturally
trusts in God and serves Him.    By their answers they
undertake the solemn responsibility to take care that it shall
be so.

There remains one objection to this view of the grace of
baptism, which at first sight seems very serious.    It is that,
as a matter of fact, these results do not follow upon baptism ;

it is sadly true that, in the words of the Article, " this infection of nature doth remain, yea in them that are regenerated." But it is important to notice the nature of this difficulty, for it is one, not of theory, but of practice. Our problem from the first has been an intellectual or theoretical problem ; we found ourselves faced with the fact that we habitually express our belief in the power of baptism to do away with original sin, and we feared lest this should be merely an inherited superstition of which no reasonable account could be given. . The argument of this essay has been an attempt to show that so far from this being the case, original sin is a reality which must be reckoned with, and that in baptism the Church applies the treatment which it needs. The reason of its failure is due to the comparative failure of the Church to live up to its ideal and its creed ; the real basis of our intellectual difficulty is a practical difficulty, and it is worth while to have discovered this to be the case. In doing so we recognise that the doctrine of Baptismal Regeneration is parallel to the other articles of the Creed which deal with the Church, in all of which there is a similar difficulty, owing to the contrast between the ideal of the Church and its actual life.

# IX.  SACRAMENTS

In his brilliant little historical study of Christian sacramental theology [1] Canon Lilley has recently shown how
sacraments (like religion, and indeed life in general) exist in
practice before attempts are made to think out the theology
they imply.  As philosophy is man's attempt, continually
renewed, to understand the life he is already living, it is
inevitable that from time to time men should try to interpret
particular practices in the light of their general convictions
about the meaning of life.  In this essay the Christian sacraments will first be considered as religious practices in relation
to the Christian life as a whole, and secondly as matters
deserving of philosophical discussion.

## I

Religion, at any rate in its more developed forms, in which
its nature most clearly appears, may be described as expressing
man's claim to exercise personal relations with the Eternal
Source of all being.  In the Christian religion these personal
relations are regarded after a special manner through the
influence of faith in the doctrines of the Incarnation and the
Trinity.

In the Fourth Gospel Jesus Christ is reported to have said
to His disciples : " It is expedient for you that I go away : for
if I go not away, the Comforter will not come unto you ; but
if I depart, I will send him unto you." [2]  Looking back over
the history of those disciples in the light of the change that
came over them on the day of Pentecost, we are enabled to
some extent to enter into the meaning of those words.  They

[1] *Sacraments : A Study of Some Moments in the Attempt to define their Meaning
for Christian Worship* (New York : The Macmillan Company, 1929).
[2] Jn. xvi. 7.

had followed their Master in the days of His flesh, and had
grown to believe in Him as the expected Messiah of their
people, but they had never really understood what that
messiahship meant as He saw it Himself from His own point
of view.   His arrest and execution had severely tested their
faith in Him, but it had been restored by His appearances
after the Resurrection.   But still they did not enter into His
mind and understand.   They had no message to preach, no
gospel; all that they could do was to wait about from one
appearance to the next, and they were still asking such
questions as " Lord, dost thou at this time restore the kingdom
to Israel ? " [1]   Even after the last of those appearances, when
He had left them in such a way as to show them that it was to
be the last, they waited about for something else to happen,
without insight and without initiative.

Whatever may have been the exact form of the outward
events of the first Whitsun Day, there can be little doubt of its
inward meaning.   Those two words, insight and initiative,
give the clue.   The men who had had no gospel to preach,
and no motive for preaching it, now had a gospel and preached
it with vigour.   Much as they had still to learn, they had
taken " the first step which counts."   They were inspired to
share their Master's insight into the meaning of His earthly
life, and to continue the work that He had come to do.

It is small wonder that in the days of His flesh our Lord
should have seen the necessity of His leaving His disciples in
order that they should come thus to share His own way of life
on earth.   Anyone with some experience of teaching knows
the over-docile pupil, who holds up his mind to be fed with a
spoon, and long after he ought to be standing on his own legs
and sharing with his erstwhile teacher in the search for truth
keeps coming back to ask to be told some more.   Christ's
ambition for His disciples was that they should come to share
His way of life on earth ; that they, like Him, should go
through life finding and doing the Father's will by the guidance and in the strength of the Spirit.

Among those who came to share in the Christian way of
life, St. Paul saw deeply into its meaning, and used to describe
it the metaphor of adoption : " Ye received the spirit of

[1] Acts i. 6.

adoption, whereby we cry, Abba, Father." [1]  As a child may be adopted to share in the already existing social life of a family on earth, so the Christian is adopted to share in the already existing social life of the Blessed Trinity.  To vary the figure, as a family on earth may extend its operations by the emigration of some of its members overseas, the life of Christ and His followers is, as it were, the extension of the social life of the Godhead to be lived among men on earth. The Christian looks out on the world around Him from within the social life of the Blessed Trinity, seeking in the power of the Spirit and with the companionship of the Son to do the Father's will.  This is the " eternal life " of the Johannine writings, and the " new and living way " of the Epistle to the Hebrews.  The spiritual relationship between God and man in Christ is a unique fact, indescribable in terms of anything else.  The language of Christian devotion attempts to dwell on different aspects of it by the use of varying metaphors.  The metaphysical unity signified by speaking of membership in Christ's body is not allowed to obscure the personal relationship implied by thinking of Him as our Elder Brother.

It is notoriously difficult to disentangle the religious from the philosophical point of view ; nevertheless the attempt must be made, and the question whether it is possible to conceive a relationship in which Christ both metaphysically constitutes and personally communes with the human soul must be reserved for discussion later on.  What we are now concerned to notice is that for religion the essence of the Christian life is the companionship of Christ in the service of the Father, and that the Christian sacraments are incidents in that way of life, apart from which setting they have no meaning.  It is this which enables two persons, while differing in their views as to the mode of Christ's presence in the Eucharist, to kneel side by side and hold communion with Him.  What they are interested in is meeting their living Lord and Master, and the question of how He comes is lost sight of in the joy of remembering who He is.

He is that same Lord whose character is made known to us in the Gospel records of His life in the flesh.  For this

[1] Rom. viii. 15.

reason it is impossible to enter into the full richness of the Christian life if sacramental religion is divorced from the study of the Bible and set over against it as an adequate substitute. There is a kind of fourfold rhythm in the Christian life, which needs to be observed. Faced by the complex problems of his life in the world a man is driven back to seek God's guidance in prayer and sacrament. But he will not find these fully if the word " God " means to him merely a vague and unsubstantial perfection ; he must turn to a Being of definite mind and character, in some degree known to him. So the attempt to find God in prayer and sacrament drives him to the study of the character of Christ in the Gospels. This study produces a desire personally to meet the Lord whose character he has been learning to know better, and coming back again to meet Him in prayer and sacrament with new insight into His character the Christian finds himself sent forth with new light and strength to face the problems of his daily life.

Again, to one who weaves together his Gospel study and his sacramental worship, every approach to the altar becomes a challenge to his daily life. As he learns to know more and more of the mind and character of his Lord, he becomes more vividly aware of what it means to meet in Person One who can say to him, " Ye have not yet resisted unto blood, striving against sin." The challenge of meeting that Personality, while it humiliates, yet makes it impossible to give up in despair. The challenge must be met and the new start made. There can be no giving up of the battle in the company of the Crucified.

In all probability a great deal of indifference to sacramental religion is due to ignorance of the fact that the way to build it up is not by study of sacramental doctrine but by study of the character of Christ. There are to-day among the laity many men and women who need to be taught how to make use of the aid provided by modern critical and historical studies so as to read the Gospels intelligently and learn to know better the character of their Lord. They need this in order that their sacramental life may be enriched, and no amount of instructions on the mode of God's sacramental activity will take its place. Religious thought moves naturally in the dramatic language of personal relations, and for the purposes of religion it is the personal communion with the living Lord that matters, the Lord who takes little children in His arms in Baptism, who in Absolution says to the penitent sinner " Go in peace," who commissions His ministers at their ordination and deepens His mystical union with us in Holy Communion. Religion can flourish in the practice of these things without there being so much as a suspicion that there are serious difficulties and controversies concerning the theology and the philosophy they involve. It is necessary that these problems should be discussed, and that in every generation the question should be raised anew how it is possible in the light of our growing knowledge to continue our inherited religious practices. It is necessary that those who go out to preach the Christian religion should be trained to appreciate its theological and philosophical implications ; and what follows may be regarded as an attempt to help towards making this possible for the present generation. Unfortunately, too often the result of the training is to lead men to preach the theology rather than the practice based upon it, to preach in terms of philosophical theory rather than in terms of personal communion with God—and then, perhaps, in violent reaction to deny the need of practice being grounded in true theory at all. Then on the one hand religion withers, and on the other obscurantism flourishes.

For the practice of the Christian religion sacraments are incidents in a life of personal communion with God made possible by man being taken by adoption to share the sonship of Christ in the social life of the Blessed Trinity. How does such a view stand in the light of philosophical reflection ?

## II

We may first consider, with reference to human life apart from religion, the relation between personal and what may be called ontological relations. It is instructive here to notice that personal relations arise as a further development on the basis of already existing physical relationships. This has been realised with growing clearness by such thinkers as Bernard Bosanquet, A. S. Pringle-Pattison, and S. A.

Alexander; and has been set forth perhaps most clearly by the last of these in his discussion of the grounds of our awareness of the existence of one another.[1] The "taking time seriously," which is the characteristic note of present-day thought, of which much has already been said in the two essays on Freedom,[2] has led to a revolution in our view of the nature of this universe of space and time. For the old picture of a vast area containing a number of things moving hither and thither within the area as a result of mutually exchanging shares in the area's constant total supply of energy, we are substituting the picture of a single stream of energy moving ever onward in one direction only, from past to future, and ever devising in the course of its progression fresh varieties of creature through which to manifest its activities. At the sub-human level this stream of energy was already expressing itself through living creatures moving in herds, and human life represents a further development in which creatures as individuals come to conscious awareness of what they already are, members of a society of individuals whose existence is grounded in one life stream which constitutes them each and all. Thus personal relationships cannot be set over against physical relationships as though that which is one cannot also be the other. There are no personal relationships except those which are the awareness of a fuller meaning in what are already physical relationships.

In order that there may be a meaning at all in any of these relationships the whole process which constitutes the universe must be regarded as expressive of purpose. This is, of course, the question of theism; the theist believes that the moving stream of energy which constitutes the fundamental reality of the spatio-temporal universe is purposive energy intelligently directed towards the fulfilment of the intelligible will of its author and source, eternal God. Through art, learning, moral insight, and personal communion God gives to man glimpses of His nature and His will, and enables man to interpret the meaning of that process which has brought him into being, in which he is called to be a co-operative agent.

[1] *Space, Time and Deity* (Macmillan, 1927), book iii., chap. i.
[2] Above, Essays IV and V.

We may now examine the distinction often drawn between what are commonly called " the natural world " and " the spiritual world." Whether or no the two phrases are justifiable ones does not now matter; the point to be made is that in the light of what has been said the distinction they are meant to convey should be stated as follows. What we should mean by spiritual is " intelligently purposive," and what we should mean by " natural " is " passively functioning without awareness of the purposive meaning of the activity." Thus that stream of energy which constitutes the spatio-temporal universe is, *taken as a whole*, a spiritual reality because, in itself and in all its emergent embodiments, sub-human and human, it is the expression of the intelligent purpose of God. But when considered, not from the standpoint of God whose purpose it expresses, but from a standpoint within itself, it is at the sub-human level " the natural world." At that level the creatures function according to the immanent purpose of God working in and through them, of which they are unaware. But men and women are capable of understanding the meaning of their existence, of intelligently purposive individual activity. Hence in them there emerge those most significant things in the course of creation —individual spiritual creatures.

This way of defining spirituality enables us to do justice to the truth that there may be spiritual wickedness arising from misuse of the capacity of purposive intelligence. Nevertheless it would be foolishly pedantic to insist on abandoning such language as that which, in speaking of " a spiritually minded man," is clearly understood to mean one who is good and not evil. Moreover, goodness seems an inadequate word for what is meant by " spiritually minded." The truth which this use of language indicates is surely this. In the life of God are riches far beyond our present comprehension. His purpose, the creative purpose which informs that stream of energy which constitutes the spatio-temporal universe, is that men and women shall come as free co-operative agents to share in that life, and to them He communicates in the process of time fresh treasures from His inexhaustible richness. These are treasures which only the intelligently purposive can receive. It may be that a man will reject them; but, by thus misusing his spirituality instead of passing on to its fulfilment, he is rightly regarded rather as a disgrace to his spirituality than as the typical man of spiritual mind. For to become a citizen of the spiritual world as distinguished from the natural world is for man not the end but the beginning; his intelligently purposive nature enables him to receive the revelation of God in Christ. In that personal co-operation the natural is not to be ousted but to be transformed into the perfect vehicle for the spiritual, until man in Christ, redeemed and wholly possessed by the Spirit of God, fulfils his adoption into the divine social life of the Blessed Trinity.

Human life has two aspects. Viewed from below we see man striving upwards to achieve his true selfhood and to build the city of God; viewed from above we see God communicating to man his true selfhood and the New Jerusalem coming down from heaven. As in our human life God's providence works through the laws of nature and the grace-controlled actions of our fellow-men [1] to provide us with the material out of which our selfhood is created, so in our spiritual life we grow by becoming that which God gives us to be ourselves. In this relationship we move towards the climax of our development, and, as before, the personal communion is based on an ontological community of nature. But whereas the personal communion of man with man is based on their parallel sharing of a nature common to all, in the communion of man with God, God communicates to man the share in His nature which enables man to know and love and serve and worship Him. It is God's by nature, and man's by God's gift. Thus at some particular stage of his progress God may have given to a man more of that which is to be the basis of his communion with God than he is at the time consciously aware of. Conscious personal relationship to God is for man not a mode of union with Him alternative to an unconscious sharing of His nature; it is only possible if there be a wider and deeper prior sharing of His nature of which he may become aware in the growth of his conscious selfhood.

As spiritual life is intelligently purposive life, so a

[1] See above, Essay V.

spiritual body is the organ of self-expression of a spiritual life. A man's natural body becomes his spiritual body by being used as the organ for the expression of his intelligently purposive life. The body must be an organ appropriate to the environment in which the life is to be expressed. If God is to fulfil His purpose of communicating to man a share in His own life, that purpose must find an embodiment through which to express itself in this world. From this point of view the laws of nature, the inspired insight of scientist, philosopher, and prophet, and the words in which they proclaim their discoveries, may all be regarded as embodying the purpose of God. In every case God's prior act of giving the body precedes man's appropriation of it. The laws of nature, our physical bodies, our glimpses of beauty, truth, and goodness in accordance with which we may try to control those laws and order those bodies, are all embodiments of God's purpose, organs of His self-expression appropriate to the world of human minds wherein He wills to make Himself known by His acts. Only if He has made us His creatures can we come to know ourselves to be His creatures and thus co-operate in the making of ourselves as the creatures He wills us to be. The whole process is illuminated by the Incarnation, wherein we see the divine life embodied in the human life of Jesus Christ, and man's appropriation of God's gift of divine sonship made possible by God's prior act of self-expression in the course of human history—an act whereby He does not merely make Himself known to us but communicates to us a sonship which we may realise by discovering that He has already constituted us His sons in Christ.

The Christian way of life is based on an act of faith which accepts Jesus of Nazareth as God living on earth under human conditions in order to initiate on earth that new relationship between God and man wherein man shares by adoption in the social life of the divine Trinity. This act of faith must be taken for granted as the setting for a discussion of sacraments, and cannot be dealt with further here.[1] In our natural

[1] I have discussed it to some extent in my contribution to *Essays on the Trinity and the Incarnation* and in *And Was Made Man*. The fullest treatment of it in modern times known to me is in L. S. Thornton : *The Incarnate Lord* (Longmans, Green & Co., 1928).

birth we do not begin to live, but pass from living under the conditions of uterine existence into the environment wherein we may grow to knowledge of ourselves as members of the world of men and women. In our baptismal rebirth we are not magically and momentarily transformed at once into perfected new creatures of another kind, but are again initiated into new conditions of existence, into the fellowship of those who share by adoption in the sonship of Christ. As in the one case, so in the other, the first step is something done in and through the individual concerned, of which he may be completely unaware. But the time comes when as an individual he learns what has been going to the making of him. We grow by discovering what we already are, and by directing the further development in the light of what we discover.

The Christian way of life is on man's part a response to God's calling him to enter upon this new relationship to Himself. The sacrament is an incident in this calling and response, and has no meaning—indeed, is non-existent— outside its setting. Let us consider the bearing on this of our statement of the distinction between the so-called natural and spiritual worlds. What is spiritual does not differ from what is natural by being made, so to speak, of a different kind of stuff. The spiritual world is the world of intelligent purpose, and that which embodies and expresses intelligent purpose is spiritual, no matter what it is "made of." If, therefore, the Church of God, in His name and carrying out His will, "consecrates" water for the baptising of new members into its fellowship, that water becomes "spiritual" in the only sense in which the word has any discoverable meaning. It is spiritual because it embodies and expresses an intelligent purpose in the personal relationship between God and man, just as the spatio-temporal universe as a whole is spiritual because it embodies the immanent purpose of its Creator. The sacraments, it must be said once again, are incidents in the social intercourse of God and men. As elements in that whole the water of Baptism and the bread and wine of the Eucharist, being instinct with God's redeeming purpose and our response, become charged with spiritual significance. As elements in that whole they

are as different from water, bread, and wine elsewhere as the
atmospheric vibrations produced by a symphony are different
from vibrations unregulated for the expression of purpose.

When we speak of the bread and wine of the Eucharist
as being " consecrated " to become the Body and Blood of
Christ, we do not mean to say that they cease to be made of one
kind of stuff and begin to be made of another, or that from
henceforth they are made of two kinds of stuff at once.    That
would be to imagine them transformed into the corpse of a
dead Christ.    But it is the presence of the living Lord which
gives its whole meaning to the service, and the value we set
on the sacrament depends on our faith that it is His will to
come among us in this way, as it was His will to walk on earth
in the body born at Bethlehem.    What makes a thing the
body of any person is not the material of which it is made, but
the fact that it is the means appropriate to the environment in
which he expresses himself.    When the Person is Christ and
the environment the society of believers, the means chosen
by the One and accepted by the others are His Body and Blood
in the only sense in which the words can mean anything at all.
And the full sense in which they are His Body and Blood is
that in which He wills to use them as such, not that in which
we are aware of their significance.    Once again, they must be
what He wills them to be before we can discover what they
are ; and at any moment our discovery may be partial and
incomplete.

The sacramental system stands for the truth that in true
religion the prior activity is God's, and man's part is to respond.    God incarnate called His disciples and sent them forth
to gather in others to share the new life in Him.    Either by
actual arrangement while with them in the flesh, or through
the guidance of His companionship in the Spirit afterwards,
He gave them certain ceremonies whereby they should unite
to make progress in their relationship to Him.    Thus the
individual comes into a society in which his own spiritual
development is of a richer content than he is consciously
aware of in his own subjective development.    He hears the
invitation " Come unto Me," and obeys the command
" Do this in remembrance of Me."    As he comes and does he
discovers more and more of what God has been doing and is

doing in, for, and through him ; and presses on towards the consummation of his development when he shall " know even as he is known."

<h1 style="text-align:center">III</h1>

To view the sacraments as incidents in the social intercourse of God and His people has certain implications to which attention may be drawn.

First, they have their place in that extension of the divine social life to embrace human beings while living here on earth. They are means by which man may grow in the realisation of His fellowship with God. The word " realisation " comes into its own in this statement, for, as has been urged over and over again, it is by becoming aware of the truth about himself and consciously appropriating it that man grows to the fullness of his capacities as a person ; through the discovery he can be made real in his selfhood. As means they are secondary to the end, which is the realised life of communion with God in Christ, and we look forward to a consummation in which God will no longer need to accommodate Himself to our spatio-temporal conditions of existence in order to make known to us the truth of our relationship to Him. Are they, here on earth, necessary means without which man cannot find communion with God ? We have no sufficient knowledge of the conditions of communion between God and man to assert that this must be so, and the empirical evidence seems clearly to show that it is not. There have been, and are, far too many men and women whose non-sacramental lives bear clear witness to their communion with God, who seem to achieve without those means the end which they exist to secure.[1] I can see no reason why this fact should diminish our estimate of the value of the sacramental system as the normal framework of the individual Christian life. Our task has been to try to interpret its meaning where it does exist. Even if it be but one of God's methods in His education of mankind in the knowledge, love, and service of Himself, it is not to be despised on that account.

Secondly, to view the sacraments as incidents in the social life of communion between God and man saves us from

<hr>

[1] See below, Essay XI, p. 160.

bothering our heads over certain questions which at times have caused distress to Christian minds. If there is no sense in asking what a sacrament is except as an incident in that intercourse, why ask? Suppose, for example, that in a celebration of the Holy Communion a portion of the consecrated Host fall to the ground and be eaten by a mouse. Does that mouse eat "the Body of the Lord," or does it not? If the answer to the question depended on an analytical definition of the crumb in terms of what it is " made of," there might be some point in raising the question. But the crumb is now a different crumb, being no longer a factor in the communion of God and man. It is between God and man that spiritual relationships can obtain, not between God and mice; and it is only within the context of spiritual relationships that bread can be charged with spiritual significance so as to become the Body of Christ. In the terminology of certain modern thinkers, the relations in which the eucharistic elements stand to their context are " internal relations," that is to say, relations which enter into their being and make them what otherwise they would not be. The religious truth corresponding to this might be expressed by saying that in the Eucharist the living Christ takes the elements offered in obedience to His command and uses them for His Body for the purpose of uniting His followers to Himself; so far as we can tell He has no such intention with regard to mice. Moreover, though reverence demands that we take all possible care to avoid accidents, it is morbid to think of our living Lord as being so imprisoned in that which He is using for His own purposes as to be desecrated against His will by a mouse. That way madness lies.

These thoughts lead directly to the third subject I wish to mention here, the very vexed question of what are called " extra-liturgical devotions to the Blessed Sacrament." Is it, or is it not, justifiable to reserve the consecrated elements as the Body and Blood of Christ so that they become a spatio-temporal focus of worship offered to Him? In the light of what has been said, it is clear that the answer to this question does not depend on whether the consecrated elements are now, in virtue of what they are " made of," some kind of " spiritual reality " in which our Lord is, so to speak, bound to remain. It depends on whether it is His will that in the social life of the redeemed community we should use the sacrament for this purpose. The spiritual life is the life of intelligent purpose, and man engages in no activity more intelligently purposive than the worship of Christ, provided that it is always remembered that He who is worshipped is the Christ whose character is shown forth in the Gospels to be a continual challenge to the worshipper's life. If it is in accordance with His will that we should foster such worship by this use of the sacrament, it is right to do so, and in that case the practice will be a spiritual one free from any taint of superstition or magic.

Is this His will? The question is not an easy one, and belongs more properly to the discussion of Authority than to this essay on sacramental religion.[1] It is impossible to believe that the full detailed content of our Lord's will for us is exhaustively revealed in His recorded utterances in the flesh, and in the present state of Christendom it is impossible to point to any organ of the Church which can be accepted as the infallible instrument for determining His will from generation to generation. Meanwhile life goes on, decisions have to be made for purposes of action, and some practical *modus vivendi* accepted. In the Anglican Communion as at present constituted it is, I believe, the duty of the bishops to consult together as Fathers in God and determine for the Church as a whole in general the policy which is to be followed as the fulfilment of Christ's will for us, and the duty of each diocesan bishop to issue regulations for the guidance of those within his jurisdiction. In doing this they will call for the advice of the best theologians the Church can produce and, in regard to the problem at present under consideration, will bear in mind the danger of encouraging ignorant superstition on the one hand and of discouraging genuine worship and devotion on the other.

What contribution this essay can make towards the solution of this vexed question can best be stated in a negative form. Whatever regulations a bishop may issue for his diocese, there would seem to be no adequate grounds arising from the philosophy of sacraments to justify disobedience to them. The decision that, so far as we can tell, it is Christ's will to use sacramental means for the purpose of uniting us to

[1] See Essay X, below.

Himself in the service of Holy Communion and not otherwise does not involve disbelief in the fullest possible objectivity of His sacramental presence in that use. The further step of deciding that, so far as we can tell, it is the will of Christ to use the reserved sacrament for the purpose of uniting to Himself the sick and those who cannot be present at the time of the consecration, implies precisely the same theology. As for the use of the reserved sacrament as a focus for our worship of Christ apart from acts of communion, if we believe that this is in accordance with His will, there is no magic or superstition necessarily present in the practice; if we believe this not to be in accordance with His will, there is no irreverence in abstaining from it. And on this particular matter at the present time I believe that there is more to be gained than lost by allowing the bishops, as the properly constituted authorities of the Church and our Fathers in God, to be the determinants of what " we " believe to be the will of our Lord.

So, for all our attempt to philosophise, we come back to where we started, the religious point of view from which all sacraments are seen to be grounded in the activity of the living God. What, from this point of view, is meant by such a phrase as " the real objective presence of Christ in the sacrament of Holy Communion " ? It means that what is of most importance in that service is not what I am consciously aware of at the moment, but what He is doing. He has bidden me to come to Him with penitence and faith—not to feel, but to do. Suppose that I have done my best in preparation to examine my conscience and ask God's forgiveness for what needs it, and now show my faith by coming once again to entrust my life to Him. Suppose that in spite of my best endeavours I cannot in the service overcome my sleepiness, or the coldness of my heart. Is Christ asleep because I am sleepy? Is His heart cold because I cannot feel? Thank God! what I am aware of in my own life is only a little fragment of the whole—the most important fragment indeed, but only important as that which I am to bring to Him in trust that He will do in, for, and through me far more than I shall ever know on earth. Christ is not asleep because I am sleepy, and when there are problems to be faced or work to be done or temptations to be met, I may go forward boldly in the power of His strength made mine.

# X.  AUTHORITY

IT is a common temptation of religious people to expect that God will miraculously preserve the domain of religious life from being subject to the conditions of life which obtain elsewhere.  Thus for a while it was thought that the writers of biblical history and biblical science were not subject to the limitations which ordinarily beset chroniclers and scientists. We have more or less learned to discount this pious expectation in our study of the Bible, but in some other directions it still seems to entangle the steps of our inquiries, and notably when we try to think about authority.  We tend, almost inevitably, to discuss the problem of authority in the Church as though it were an isolated problem peculiar to Church life, to be decided entirely by reference to ecclesiastical arguments and precedents.  It will be the aim of this essay to inquire whether light may not be shed on the question of authority in the Church by relating some of the problems it involves to similar problems elsewhere.

## I

In the first place, it is well worth remembering that, as Aristotle remarked long ago, in every inquiry we have to be content with that degree of accuracy of which the subject-matter admits.  To think that God must have given a final revelation, in clear-cut black-and-white terms easily understood by all, of the problem of authority in religious matters which He has not given in similar problems elsewhere is a symptom of the malady from which we are trying to escape. It may be that the absence of a final solution is one of the conditions prescribed by God for the development of human life in religion as elsewhere, and that, as so often, the end of

our immediate inquiry will not be the solution of our difficulties, but the discovery where the true difficulties lie.   If we
can pare away the superficial problems and penetrate to a
recognition of one of those standing tensions which make
human life worth living, we shall have achieved a result not
wholly without value.

It is instructive to notice that the problem of authority
only arises at a somewhat developed stage of Church life, and
to observe that a similar development takes place elsewhere.
In the history of Christian thought, as in that of human
thought in general, such questions are only raised when an
attitude of reflective self-consciousness leads to a turning
away from the pursuit of knowledge to a criticism of the
organ whereby that knowledge is preserved.   In the history
of philosophy that turning-point has been well described by
Professor C. C. J. Webb in his " Studies in the History of
Natural Theology," [1] and the subsequent inquiry into the so-
called " Theory of Knowledge " is familiar to all, as it followed
its course from the impetus given by Descartes through the
work of Locke and Berkeley to the scepticism of Hume.
This provoked the reaction of Kant which led to the development of absolute idealism and has been followed in recent
times by a return to various forms of realistic epistemology.
Meanwhile the work of scientific research went on, and those
who gave themselves to it were, for the most part, neither
disturbed by those philosophers who argued that they were
pursuing a will-o'-the-wisp, nor grateful to those who tried
to show that they were discovering something of the nature
of reality.   Nor could the philosophical argument itself have
been conducted except by the use of the organ whose competence to conduct it was being questioned, and it is now
generally recognised that while a critical study of epistemology
is a necessary part of philosophical inquiry, to *substitute* it for
the attempt to discover objective truth is a futile and self-
contradictory proceeding.   In spite of the fact that physicists,
physiologists and psychologists daily increase our awareness
of our ignorance concerning how we think, we nevertheless
go on thinking and continue to believe that by doing so we
make some progress in the discovering of truth.   Moreover,

[1] Oxford University Press, 1915.   See especially pp. 147–153.

we learn to beware of the man who tries to side-track us in some inquiry by switching the discussion from the consideration of its object to that of our organs of apprehension, who will not meet us face to face and weigh the intrinsic value of our arguments, but attempts to circumvent us by describing the sub-conscious grounds of our "rationalisations," or the state of our endocrine glands.

What is the bearing of all this on the question of authority in the Church? It is to suggest that the question of authority must never be allowed to arrogate to itself more than a secondary place in our minds. The progressive discovery of truth, which underlies the development of Christian doctrine, went on before anyone thought of raising the question by what organ of the corporate body it was discovered, and now that the question has been raised there is no reason why we should suspend the prior activity until we can find its answer. Important as the question is, its obscurity must not be made an excuse for refusing to face squarely the problems which arise in the relations of God and man.

## II

Another allied problem in a different field which it is worth while to consider is the problem of sovereignty as it is discussed in political philosophy by such writers (to name a few at random) as Hobbes, Locke, Rousseau, T. H. Green, Bernard Bosanquet, W. E. Hocking and H. J. Laski. Where does sovereignty reside? Is it the prerogative of the king as one born to rule by divine right? Or is it rightfully claimed by some group, those (for example) who excel in wealth or in wisdom or in courage? Moreover, four questions are here often intertwined. We may ask: (1) Where does sovereignty actually lie in general? (2) Where should sovereignty actually lie in general? (3) Where does sovereignty actually lie here and now in this community? and (4) Where should sovereignty actually lie here and now in this community? That these questions are to be distinguished from one another may be seen from the fact that a man might answer them all differently. He might, for instance, hold a position which led him to say that

(1) sovereignty in general actually resides in the hands of those elements in the community who best combine cunning and power, whereas (2) it should belong to the people at large as a whole ; (3) in this state it has been usurped by a single dictator whose cunning and power have enabled him to become supreme and (4) to suppress the institutions whereby the people ought to be exercising their sovereign rights.

For the theist the problem is simplified ; but the corollaries of the simplification are not always clearly grasped. The answers to the first two questions coincide : sovereignty both does and should belong to God.[1] Questions (3) and (4) thus become concerned with the organ or instrument for the exercise of the divine sovereignty on earth, and there is no antecedent ground for assuming that the same form of organisation will always be the right one at all times and in all places. It may be possible, moreover, to combine a genuine devotion to the democratic ideal with a recognition of the fact that a certain nation has not yet sufficiently developed as a whole in political understanding to justify the establishment of a fully democratic system of self-government.

No student of political philosophy is alarmed or surprised by the fact that the search for answers to the questions where sovereignty does and should reside on earth is unending. It is the nature of human life that such questions should have to be raised and solved anew in different times and places. That which unifies the diverse modes of government is in the beyond : it is the sovereignty of God which chooses now this and now that earthly embodiment. But here again we religious people often seem to expect that our human life in the Church shall be exempted from the conditions of all human life on earth, and to think it a scandal that there should be any *problem* of authority at all ! It is a real gain, I believe, to grasp firmly the fact that there is no antecedent ground for expecting the seat of authority in the Church to be the same element in the corporate body at all times and in all places. There may well be times when *securus iudicat orbis terrarum*, and also times when the *Vox Dei* is expressed through *Athanasius contra mundum*.

[1] See C. C. J. Webb: *In Time of War* (Oxford: Blackwell, 1918), iii., iv.

When two parties in the Church are in dispute over some question of doctrine (even though one party be an individual on trial for alleged heresy, and the other the duly constituted organ of Church government), neither is an ultimate authority. Each claims to represent the mind and will of God as made known to them; and judgment can never rightly be passed without a prayer that the earthly sentence may turn out to be such that it is ratified in heaven.

### III

The problems concerning the development of doctrine provide our next instance of the way in which questions of a wider import appear in a particular form in theological discussions. In the development of Christian doctrine, what is it that remains the same, and what is it that changes? Our temptation is to think that this is a simple question, which can be answered once and for all by some nice neat little phrase such as " the rendering explicit of what was implicit in the *depositum fidei*." In thus expecting a final answer to one of the deepest of unsolved problems we only reveal the superficiality of our own thought—like Professor John Dewey, who thinks to solve his problems by reference to " the notion of growth," thus closing the door on philosophical inquiry just where it ought to begin.[1]

The problem of being and becoming, of identity in difference, is a deep mystery wherever it is found, whether it be in the evolutionary process of creation taken as a whole, or in the growth of a single acorn into an oak. There is something that remains the same, for an acorn does not become a beech or an elm. But what is it? If a man could answer that question, one might be prepared to listen with some expectation of enlightenment to what he had to say concerning the principle of development in Christian doctrine. Meanwhile, until he appears, we had better continue to beware of apparently simple formulae employed to disguise the difficulty.

[1] See *Experience and Nature* (Chicago: Open Court Publishing Co., 1925), p. 275; and compare H. W. B. Joseph: *The Concept of Evolution* (Oxford University Press, 1924).

Undoubtedly there is an element which remains the same through all the true development of the Christian faith, and undoubtedly there are false attempts at development which have to be rejected as perversions. But by what canon the true are to be distinguished from the false is a question as yet passing the wit of man. The Christian religion is a unique thing in the world, working out its development for the first and only time in history. We are, as it were, inside the first acorn that became an oak, and how can we tell which is the right way to be going?

Negative and unsatisfactory as the results of our inquiry may so far appear, they have at least one considerable value. Now that we realise the true nature of some of the difficulties involved in the question of authority in the Church, we shall cease impatiently to demand an immediate and final solution. Out of the background of unsolved mysteries we shall seek grounds for action whereby we may walk by reasonable faith if not by sight.

## IV

There is no longer any novelty in the assertion that the words "human reason" and "divine revelation" denote neither two different methods of arriving at the same truth, nor two different methods each appropriate to discovering a different kind of truth, but the obverse and reverse sides of the one and only method of discovering truth at all. All truth is God's truth, whether it be discovered by microscope or telescope, by prophetic insight, or by any other mode of human sensitiveness working through whatever instrument it finds available. In so far as the discovery is due to God's provision of that which we learn about Him, it comes through divine revelation; in so far as it is apprehended by us through our human capacity for grasping it, it comes through the use of human reason.

But, although we can no longer set reason and revelation over against one another as has sometimes been done in the past, there is a very real distinction to be recognised which may, perhaps, be described by using the terms "general revelation" and "special revelation." Man learns through his experience of spatio-temporal particulars occurring in the history of creation, and in course of time penetrates to the interpretation of them as earthly embodiments of a stream of purposive energy proceeding from an eternal source. Indeed, he penetrates still deeper, and finds himself holding personal relations with that source of all being, whom he loves, serves and worships as God. Whence has this deeper insight come to him? Through special series of historical events occurring within the wider framework of spatio-temporal events in general, the most significant of such special series of events being the history of the Hebrew people with its culmination in the Gospel story and the development of the Christian Church.[1] If, for example, I ask myself whence I derive my convictions (*a*) that water runs downhill, and (*b*) that God's loving forgiveness is adequate to absorb the blackest sins I can conceivably commit, I regard the first as belonging to the sphere of " general revelation " and the second to that of " special revelation." To illustrate the point further, learning by special revelation may be analogous to taking a special course in university (or other) education. A man who has made a special study of some department of medicine thereby knows more of some things than his fellow-men who have not shared his experience ; he becomes, as we say, a specialist. Similarly, a man who has entered into that knowledge of God which He has given us in the historical development of the Christian religion has, *as a matter of fact*, received a special revelation which others can only share by sharing with him in the method of discovery.

It is a commonplace of traditional theology to state that the full richness of God's being is not exhausted in what He reveals of His nature to man. To us who, in this generation, are learning to " take time seriously," and to regard the history of human development as the communication by God to man of an increasing insight into and share in His own life, it is clear that at no moment is the full content of that which is to be given comprised in revelation-up-to-date. The incarnation of God in Jesus Christ was the initiation of

---

[1] Cp. A. N. Whitehead : *Religion in the Making* (New York, 1926), pp. 47 ff. ; and C. C. J. Webb : *Studies in the History of Natural Theology* (Oxford, 1915), pp. 29-32.

a new stage in that process of God's giving and man's receiving, a stage in which from the beginning there lies the potentiality of the fulfilment of the whole purpose of God for man ; but the full meaning of God's self-revelation of Himself to man in Christ will only become possessed by man when in the course of time His Church has entered into it.

By recognising the distinction between special revelation and general revelation, as drawn above, we would seem to catch a glimpse of the plan devised by God for the education of His Church. God is one, but He reveals Himself to us in different ways. As a result of this there come actions and reactions, and often a state of tension, between our apprehensions of Him received in different modes of His self-manifestation. In the passing of time it does not always happen that our development along the one path keeps step with that along the other. An " age of faith " may need to be followed by an age of scientific progress, and then the " faith " may find that it needs to readjust its own understanding of itself before it is ready to reinspire the failing optimism of disillusioned science. Sometimes the one field, and sometimes the other, is that in which the advance is being made, and then there is often friction before, on one side or other, the leeway is made up. This friction is God's spur to our mental inertia, goading us on to enter into the fuller possession of what He has in store for us.

If this be so, then it is one of the most important duties of the Christian Church to be always on the look-out to discover what in the field of general revelation will illuminate and develop our understanding of our faith. We have, indeed, to hold and guard the content of our special revelation, to bear witness to that element of identity which must persist through all the changes, but (like the talent in the parable) it is not to be buried in the ground or hidden in a napkin, but to grow by trafficking in the commerce of human thought.

From this point of view, the question of authority in the Church wears a slightly different aspect from that which we have already considered. We may now think of the Church as a society on earth entering by the use of its reason into the revelation which God is giving it. The question now is, which of the possible claimants can rightly be recognised as the reason of the Church for the fulfilment of this task? Is it to be the reason of any one individual, or of some group, or of the whole body? All three methods have been tried, but none, so far as I am aware, with success. The reversal of its decisions in succeeding generations appears to be an inevitable Nemesis that overtakes every officially infallible organ of humanity appointed for the discovery of truth. Perhaps our last and fiercest temptation, as churchmen, is the temptation to cling to the delusion that, because we are the sons of God, we may cast ourselves down from the pinnacle of our theological edifice, upborne by angels for whose aid the mathematician and the physiologist may plead, but will plead in vain.

## V

The problem of sovereignty, the problem of identity in difference, the problem of the validity of human reason—here are three problems which are always with us in secular philosophy. Progress comes not by evading them, or shutting our eyes to them, but by wrestling with them as they recur from age to age embodied in concrete situations. Within the Church these problems present themselves in special forms, and we delude ourselves if we expect to be exempt from the task of wrestling as our brothers wrestle elsewhere. So far as the " church militant here on earth " is concerned, we must not ask for a final, once-for-all solution of any one of these problems in terms of a neat formula to be used at all times and in all places as a criterion of justifiable sovereignty, of true identity, or of infallible pronouncement. It is not the authority which guarantees the content of its utterance, but the content of the utterance which proves or disproves the authority.

But what is to prove or disprove the content of the utterance? The motto of present-day thought—that we are learning to "take time seriously"—gives the answer. "Time will show." If this appears cold comfort, it is at any rate consoling to reflect that, in spite of all theories and formulae, it describes the method by which the Church has actually lived and grown, whether it knew it or not. It was prescribed many years ago by an unknown writer in the book Deuteronomy,[1] and it survives in the teaching given to students of dogmatic theology in our theological colleges to-day. When it is asked what constitutes an oecumenical decision, the answer is that the decision must be promulgated by a constitutionally convened council of the Church and ratified by being accepted by the faithful.[2] Thus, of the decrees put forward by the Council of Nicaea in the year 325, some did and some did not attain to oecumenical authority. The process of ratification and rejection was essentially similar to that whereby in more recent years certain teachings of Bishop Colenso were first condemned by officially appointed guardians of the Anglican faith, and are now taught in every Anglican seminary. " The ratification of conciliar decisions by catholic consent " is a translation into ecclesiastical language of the maxim " Time will show."

It would probably be unwise to attempt to define with any precision the functions which should be performed by different elements in the Church, as it goes on its way down the ages learning what time has to show ; what part, for instance, is to be played by the piety of the saint, the learning of the scholar, or the administrative wisdom of the episcopate. But from empirical observation one generalisation seems to be possible as descriptive of what does as a matter of fact happen. It seems, as a general rule, to be the part of the Church as a whole in its corporate capacity to bear witness to the element of identity, of being, in the Christian faith, to conserve for the future the " revelation-up-to-date," while it is left to individual initiative to emphasise the element of difference, of becoming, to explore the untravelled realms of truth still to be revealed. Here, once again, the life of the Church is not without its parallel in other spheres. The exploration of new countries, the provision of transportation and postal service, the care of the sick, and the education of the young—these and many other public utilities usually owe their existence to private initiative and are only taken over

[1] Deut. xviii. 21, 22.
[2] Cp. T. A. Lacey on " Catholic Consent," in *Authority in the Church : A Study of Principles* (London : A. R. Mowbray & Co., 1928).

and reorganised as public concerns when they have proved their worth. It is the normal way of progress in human society that new ventures should be the work of individuals or groups who are, as it is said, " in advance of their time." Some of them will be successful, and others will be failures. As time winnows the wheat from the chaff, it is gathered into the official storehouse of the society. It is no reproach to the Church that in its official utterances it lags behind the inspired prophets of the day, so long as the prophets are encouraged to follow their inspiration, and tolerated if sometimes they prophesy somewhat wildly. Ultimately the truth will prevail, and what the truth is time will show.

But is our last word to be in praise of deified Time? God forbid! Time is not God, but God's. There would be no ground for trusting in time to show the truth were not time merely the name for that order of successiveness through which God makes Himself known to man. " Time will show " is a phrase which, rightly interpreted, means " God will show in His own time." It is a useful phrase, because it recalls us from our modern impatience which leads us to demand, like Marcion of old, that God shall do everything on a sudden, and bids us wait upon Him for the solution of our problems.

It is inevitable that from time to time there shall be tension and friction between the deliverances of special revelation and general revelation, and also between the accepted content of revelation-up-to-date and the forward-adventuring speculation of prophet or scholar. When these are in apparent conflict, what are we to do? We must renew our faith in the first article of our Creed. There is but one God, and He is the Creator of all things visible and invisible—special revelation and general revelation, truth already grasped and truth yet to be learned, these all come from Him, and in Him is to be found their reconciliation and their unity. It is the unity of God in which we put our trust, and the test of a robust faith in Him is our willingness to tolerate for a time the strain and stress of inability to reconcile apparent contradictions in our discoveries. They must continue to be felt as strains and stresses, as incentives to further effort towards that knowledge of God in which they shall be harmonised. But because our faith is faith in God the eternal giver, who still has more to give, and not in man as up to the present endowed, we shall cease to complain of the conditions of our learning and to look for some already constituted infallibly authoritative guide. Order and authority there must be in the Church, but it is such authority as is needed for practical purposes to enable the Church to continue pressing onward in the exploration of all that God has to give in the way in which God wills us to receive it. There are times when for the good of the whole body the headstrong individual must be checked by the authority of " the powers that be," and there are times when the " powers that be " must recognise the voice of one who speaks with authority and not as the scribes. Only in each situation as it arises can the question be decided where on this occasion the authority is to be found. Yet our conclusion is not the advocacy of chaotic anarchy, for by our faith we trust in the guidance of Him who is the source of all authority, believing with the poet Lowell that

> " Standeth God within the shadow,
> Keeping watch above His own."

# XI. THE REUNION OF CHRISTENDOM

## I. Presuppositions

### (a) *Philosophical Presuppositions*

ONE of my earliest recollections of events in the world at large is of the controversy on religious education which invaded English politics in the year 1906. It impressed itself with all the force of a new interest on the mind of a boy just beginning to discover for himself the world of politics. Moreover, to a Pauline of those days the name of Bishop Knox of Manchester was well known as that of a famous O.P. and the author of many " remedies," while to one brought up at home in the traditions of the Oxford Movement Lord Halifax was *magnum et venerabile nomen*. Why my elders should regard it as so significant that Bishop Knox and Lord Halifax should unite to speak from the same platform I could not altogether understand ; but I gathered that they had done so, and that it marked the importance of the cause for which they stood. The more picturesque episode of the Bishop marching through London at the head of his Lancashire Sunday schools helped to stamp the impression of the controversy indelibly on my memory, though what it was all about I had probably no very clear idea at the time.

Four or five years later came the beginning of serious

study of philosophy, and the introduction through Plato to the problem of universal and particular. I well remember the day when, during an Oxford vacation, I was walking through Surrey fields with a school friend who had been articled to study law in London while I had gone to the university. As was our wont, we expounded to one another the principles of law and philosophy, and discussed in their light the world of men and things. Our conversation turned on the education controversy of our schooldays, and there came to me in a sudden flash the bearing on it of that problem of universal and particular which just then filled my mind. Further reflection on the matter has only served to deepen the conviction that in that moment of insight I had grasped a principle of prime importance for the discussion of Christian unity.

The controversy of 1906 was concerned with the teaching of the Christian religion in the State-supported and State-aided schools of England. The champions of the Church of England demanded that the children of Church parents in all schools, and the children of all who did not contract out in schools on a Church foundation, should be taught the religion of the Church Catechism and the Book of Common Prayer. Nonconformists objected to the payment of taxes to support the teaching of a form of Christianity in which they did not believe, and demanded that there should be taught the common undenominational Christianity so far as it was agreed on by all. Driven by the heat of controversy into extreme positions, one party denied that there was any such thing as this common Christianity, the other asserted that there was, and that it could be described and imparted to children as " simple Bible teaching."

The truth surely is that both parties were driven into error by failing to grasp the same point, the relation of universal and particular which pervades all our experience in this universe of space and time. We know the nature of triangularity, but we can only actualise it in space and time as equilateral, isosceles, or scalene. In each of these we can recognise a unity which transcends the particular instance and is capable of embodiment in mutually exclusive forms, but which cannot be actualised in its fullness in any earthly form. So the fact that Christianity, in order that it may be lived and taught, must be embodied in some actual way of faith and practice, does not necessarily imply that any one such way is exhaustive of its possibilities of embodiment in human lives. It may be that the unity of Christianity is so rich ánd glorious a thing that no one way of living it is adequate to its full embodiment on earth.

This theoretical possibility seems to me to be empirically verified as the truth of the matter by further experience of the actual facts of Christian life. I was born and bred, as I have said, in the traditions of the Oxford Movement, and to me religion which centres in the worship of the Altar and surrounds that with the recitation of the daily offices, the regular ministry of priestly absolution, and all that goes with these will in all probability always be the way of life in which I shall be most at home, in which I shall most naturally find for myself the presence of God and attempt to present it to others. But (not to go beyond the confines of the Anglican communion) from the days when as an undergraduate I shared in a small way in the activities of Dr. Stansfeld and his associates in Bermondsey, to those later occasions when I have joined in the worship of the Church of Ireland in Ulster and have learned something of the movement known as " The First Century Christian Fellowship," I have found it impossible not to recognise in such work and worship genuine expressions of Christianity—different, indeed, from that in which I am at home, and in some ways opaque to my appreciation, yet ways as genuinely integral to Christianity as my own, without which the life of our Church would be grievously impoverished.

Nor is it possible, as some seem to think, to regard one of these ways of life as inclusive of the others, and each other as an incomplete form of the one. There is a totally different character of the life, a different *ethos* ; the one is, so to speak, as isosceles as the other is scalene. The full richness of the Christian way of life cannot be exemplified in the life of any one man or in any one group of men. It requires a body articulated into complementary members, each making its own contribution to the balanced harmony of the whole.

Another way of approach which leads to the same conclusion is provided by raising the question : " Is it conceivable that the whole world will ever become either Catholic or Protestant ? " Some enthusiastic adherents of either side believe that it will, and that it is their own side which is destined to absorb the other. But the more I learn of each the less I am able to share the sublime faith of either ; and it is remarkable how hard it is to persuade many people really to face the question at all. When it is faced, the possible alternatives seem to be two : either the ultimate goal of efforts after the reunion of Christendom will be to resolve the present multiplicity of churches and sects into two great bodies, eyeing one another in hostile rivalry to the end of time, or all must find their place in a larger whole, whose richness depends on the harmony of its diverse parts. Where the actual situation demands just such a conception of unity as our philosophical reflection discovers to be most truly reasonable, we need not hesitate to choose which shall be our aim.

For the sake of simplicity I have spoken in the last few paragraphs as though Christianity requires for its earthly embodiment two ways of life, the Catholic and the Protestant. But once the point is grasped, it must be clearly understood that there is no reason why there should be two such ways and no more. One has only to think of the Society of Friends to see the possibility of a distinct third. The practical problems provided by recognising the true nature of the oneness of Christianity as a unifying principle transcending its earthly embodiments are indeed serious. To determine, for instance, what are and what are not genuine expressions of the Christian way of life is no easy task. But these, and other practical problems, must be dealt with later. It is enough for the moment to have learned that the road to unity is not by effacing the vital characteristics of various ways of Christian living into a colourless cosmopolitanism, or by expecting one to absorb the rest, but by developing each to its fullness in order that it may make its full contribution to the life of the whole body of which it is to be visibly and organically an articulated member.

## (b) *Theological Presuppositions*

Closely allied to the philosophical presuppositions, which have now been briefly sketched, are certain theological presuppositions which arise from reflection on the doctrine of the Trinity. It is not too much to say that of recent years research into the history of this doctrine, and growing familiarity with the so-called " organic " conception of unity consequent on modern biological study, have combined to revolutionise our attitude towards it and to deepen our appreciation of it. This " organic " conception leads us to think of unity not as the flat antithesis of multiplicity, but as an active principle unifying its diverse constituents in a richly articulated whole. In the early centuries of our era, when the Christian creeds were in process of formulation, the natural line for philosophical thought to follow was to contrast unity and multiplicity and to seek the One by dissolving away the diversity of the many. Thus the logical conclusion of the philosophy of the day was, as Mr. Whittaker has shown, the Neoplatonic system.[1] But philosophy must never forget that its task is not to construct a world of its own apart from the actual given world, but to seek to understand and interpret that world as it is given ; and there had been given in the Incarnation fresh material for the conception of God which required a radical revision of men's thought about Him. For the time being philosophy could make little or nothing of this new material ; it could not pass from its unitarian to a genuinely trinitarian way of thinking without a struggle. The Christian doctrine of the Trinity, so far from being (as some have supposed) an alien corruption of primitive faith by Greek metaphysics, represents Christian fidelity to the revelation given in Christ.[2] The doctrine was foisted by the Christians upon a metaphysic unable to assimilate it, as may be seen by the fact that when a metaphysical formulation of it was sought in the *Quicunque Vult*, all that could be done was to set down a list of contradictions and require acceptance of them under pain of severe spiritual penalties.

[1] T. Whittaker, *The Neo-Platonists* (Cambridge University Press, 1918).

[2] See, *e.g.*, Dr. K. E. Kirk's essay in *Essays on the Trinity and the Incarnation* (ed. Rawlinson; Longmans, Green & Co., 1928).

It is one of the miracles of Christian history that this doctrine should now, some fifteen centuries later, be re-discovered as the one truly intelligible way of thinking about God.   This cannot be discussed further here, but enough has been said to introduce the point on which I wish to dwell.

According to our human experience it is at the lowest level of life that we find the blank undifferentiated unity of the amoeba; the higher we go in the scale of life, the more richly complex are the differentiations unified in the activity of a living whole.  According to the Christian faith this thought of unity as an active principle unifying diverse elements within it is not to be regarded merely as an accident of spatio-temporal existence.   Enshrined at the heart of our thought about God is the thought of Him as the perfection of such unity as that after which we aspire on earth.   It is a unity which would be destroyed either by effacing the distinctions within it, or by impairing the love which unites them; we must neither confound the Persons nor divide the Substance.

The divine life is a social life, and the pattern after which all human social life is to be transformed.   According to the pattern there must be varieties within the social whole, united in one life by love.   It will destroy the true pattern of unity if the varieties are effaced, or the cords of unifying love broken.   The Catholic must learn to thank God for the life of his Protestant brother, and *vice versa*, each learning to appreciate the other for what he is—to appreciate him because he can make a contribution to the life of the Church which he himself cannot.

It does not need much experience of human nature to realise that this demand is one which challenges much in man that is most difficult to overcome and transform.   Of this more must be said later.   It is enough for the moment to have learned that when our vision of the reunion of Christendom is dismissed with the remark that it is " not in human nature," we may reply " Perhaps not; but it is in divine nature, and please God it shall some day be ours." For what is the Christian programme, if it be not the trans-forming of human nature after the image of the divine ?

### (c) *Religious Presuppositions*

To a superficial observer it sometimes appears as though religion, in contrast with certain other activities of man, were a peculiarly divisive factor in human life.   One may notice a brotherhood of art, of learning, of sport, and of commerce, uniting by a common interest men and women of varied races, tongues and creeds.   In contrast with these the religious world is exhibited as a byword for internecine strife and mutual hostility.

Even if attention be confined to this contrast as it appears lying on the surface of history, it is doubtful whether such an estimate of it is justified.   And when we try to look below the surface, we soon find that there are considerations which lead us to revise such a judgment.

There is another contrast between religion and such other activities of man as those noticed above, and it demands our attention.   Those activities may be described as departmental.   It is *in so far as* a man is a scholar, or an artist, or a sportsman, or engaged in commerce, that he finds a bond of brotherhood with others engaged in similar activities. But whole tracts of his life may be left outside the brotherhood—indeed, very often they are.

A man's religion can never rightly be treated as a departmental activity of life, kept strictly in its place and never allowed to interfere with other interests and activities.

> " Love so amazing, so divine,
>   Demands my soul, my life, my all."

A man's religion, if it is to be true religion and have its perfect work, must permeate and penetrate into every nook and cranny of his life.   Hence religious unity among men, if it is to be truly religious unity and have its perfect work, must permeate and penetrate every nook and cranny of their lives.   It must not be an agreement to combine for certain departmental purposes, but a genuine brotherhood in the family of God—a brotherhood in which there are no reservations, nothing kept back as incapable of sacrifice for the common good.   To kneel at the same altar rail and cut one another in the street is no true Christian intercommunion. There can be no true union of Christendom until white men, yellow men, brown men and black men, Nordics, Latins, Slavs and Mongols, Englishmen, Americans, Frenchmen and Germans, Italians, Rumanians and Bulgars, Greeks, Turks and whatsoever other varieties there be of the human race, are united in a loving brotherhood penetrating and permeating every department of life.

What is it that holds us back from this brotherhood? Is it religion? Partially, no doubt, it is ; but by no means entirely. Man did not need religion to instil into him the seeds of unbrotherliness towards his neighbours. That unbrotherliness is a sad fact, and God in Christ is striving to overcome it. Victories over it are won in this direction and that, in various departmental activities of life. But religious unity, just because it demands the most thoroughgoing victory over all in us that hinders us from loving our neighbour, is the most difficult of all to achieve, and it is not surprising that it should take longer to appear on earth than certain other less searching forms of human brotherhood.

If this be so, then the task before Christendom is not to get back to a union which once obtained and has been lost, but to press on to a union which never yet has been but some day shall be. This thought leads on to the historical questions which must occupy our next section. For the moment it is enough to suggest that there could be no more hideous caricature of Christian reunion than for a number of ecclesiastical leaders to content themselves with getting together at Lausanne or elsewhere and making an agreement for unity in a departmental activity of life called " religious."

### (d) Historical Presuppositions

The history of the world, as read by a Christian, is like the story of a great romance. The beginning is lost, and the end is not yet seen ; but there is sufficient material to enable us to catch the drift of the plot. The chief character in the story is God, and He is working out His purpose of uniting men and women in one brotherhood of love. He likes variety, and aims at a brotherhood uniting multitudinous distinct types of men and women. The beginning of the story is lost, and we grope about in the dark speculating on the origin of evil, but it is clear that when the curtain lifts men and women are not brotherly. History begins as a record of human selfishness and strife—and has not yet ceased to be so.

Nevertheless, some progress has been made. The problem before God is to keep mankind interesting by preserving alive and sharply distinct their multitudinous variety of types, and to respect and develop their freedom, so that what issues may be a brotherhood of men and women, not a stage full of puppets. The Old Testament helps us to see how He works, instilling into men's minds the ideals of those virtues without which brotherhood is impossible, then waiting patiently for men to make them their own, and always ready to help with the grace that meets their freedom more than half way.

The turning-point of the story is the Incarnation, the coming of the Prince of Peace to establish His kingdom of righteousness and love. For the time being the power of evil was too strong, and His body was broken on the cross for the healing of mankind. But He had left behind a little company of men and women to be the body through which He should continue to work on earth. At first all seemed to go well. There were, indeed, disputes and schisms incidental to the working out of a form of organisation suitable to their needs, and a formulation of their faith. But the unity of the society was not broken to any real extent.

This could not last. Such a period of internal peace was indeed necessary, but only as preparation for the task that lay ahead. It was only achieved by accepting, for the time being, a departmentalised conception of religion which could not be acquiesced in permanently. The early Christian did not permeate and penetrate his social, political, and national relationships with his Christianity; in order to be a Christian he stepped out of these into the Christian society, and left his old world unredeemed behind Him.

Under the providence of God the growth of national self-consciousness brought the issue to a head. For a while there was a state of unresolved tension, the centripetal influence of Christ in His Church resisting the centrifugal force of human antagonism. But, as before, the victory could not be won except through temporary submission to man's misuse of his freedom; as the body of Christ was broken on the Cross, so His body the Church was broken for the healing of the nations. In the resulting " confusion of the churches " the Spirit of God has never ceased to be working, as is His wont, turning all circumstances to good account, and making them minister to the fulfilment of His will.[1] The christianising of the nations, although proceeding in unchristian disunion, has served to reveal in various types the multifarious richness of the Christian way of life, and man has learned that the solution of problems of inter-racial and international relations is germane to the fulfilment of God's purpose for mankind. It is a brotherhood which preserves and harmonises these differences at which He aims, and His Church must never again aim at a unity for herself which is not unifying these. As God is interested in them, so they must be her interest as she seeks unity for herself.

In these days the Spirit of God is moving through Christendom, revealing to us the evil of our disunion, calling us to repent of it and to work for its repair. He is calling us to a greater work than we sometimes realise. He is calling us to a brotherhood of all mankind touching every department of life, and the field in which work needs to be done is wide : social, industrial, racial, and international problems all have their place in the task before us. We cannot treat Church unity as a separate problem to be solved on its own out of all relation to these various questions. We must recognise in the great desire for reunion which moves the hearts and consciences of Christian people to-day the voice of God calling upon His Church to draw men into that complete brotherhood which is His will for us. We must enlarge our vision, and frame our policies for the Church with a view to that great purpose of God for the fulfilment of which His Church has been founded and preserved.

### (e) Ecclesiastical Presuppositions

At the root of true religion lies the conviction on man's part that he has in some way been called or chosen by God.

---

[1] See above, Essay V, pp. 58–60.

Whether the religion be corporate or individual, it is the experience of belonging to a chosen people, or being a chosen person.   This is as true of every one of us as it was of Moses and the Prophets.   No one of us can claim to be the author of his own Christian faith.   Some of us were born into Christian families, and grew naturally into our inheritance of faith ; some of us came into the faith through the influence of teacher, preacher or friend.   But in every case our action was a response to the providential activity of God ; we are Christians because He has said to us, as to the disciples of old :  " Ye have not chosen me, but I have chosen you."

This conviction, which down the ages has been the root of true religion, has been subject down the ages to the temptation to give the wrong answer to the question Why am I called ?   The wrong answer is, " For my own benefit as contrasted with other people " ; the right answer is, " For the glory of God and the service of mankind."   As was once observed (perhaps somewhat maliciously), the song of the Catholic Church is not " That will be glory for me," but " Glory to God in the highest."

The point is of greater importance than at first appears. It is essentially the same as that which in an earlier essay was described as providing the *pons asinorum* of ethics.[1]   In religion it takes the form of the truth that while response to God's call is undoubtedly the way of salvation, the response must not be made *because* it is the way of salvation.   This paradox has been one of the most difficult lessons for man to learn in the course of his religious education.   The Old Testament is the record of God's attempts to teach it. Prophet after prophet had to be sent to proclaim to " the chosen people " that they must not regard their choice as a guarantee of their own unique supremacy, but as a call to be " a light to lighten the Gentiles "—that only shipwreck could be expected if they refused to care for the salvation of Nineveh equally with their own.   Failure to have learned this lesson. made it impossible for Christ to use the Jewish *ecclesia* as His instrument, and drove Him to commission a " remnant " to be the Body of His continued working on earth.   Infection of soteriological thought by the same error

---

[1] Above, Essay VI, p. 68.

led to the darker side of St. Augustine's teaching on pre-destination, and to its development in the Calvinistic system.[1]

Christianity did not come into men's minds as into a vacuum, but into minds already occupied with a world of ideas, many of which it was to transform as the years went by. In studying the history of Christian doctrine it is as important to notice the disentangling and rejection of ideas inconsistent with Christianity but at first inextricably inter-twined with men's apprehension of it, as to notice the growing appreciation of its own richness of content.[2] It has taken centuries to discard the error caused by the mistaken estimate of the meaning of God's calling, and the lesson is not yet fully learned. It is this mistaken interpretation which is the ground of that way of thinking about the Church which regards it primarily as the Ark of Salvation.

This way of thinking leads to an imaginary picture in which different Christian bodies are represented as rival ferry-boats offering would-be passengers safe transportation across the waves of this troublesome life and death to the shores of the Heavenly City. It is essential to the claims of each that it should profess to be the one official guaranteed ark, compared with which others are possibly, but doubtfully, safe vessels. The adherent of any one of them is faced by a dilemma. If he is strict about the conditions of embarkation in his vessel, he must exclude from the way of salvation many of his fellow-men because their honest convictions prevent them from accepting those conditions. If of very charity he finds himself unable to do this, he is in danger of relaxing his conditions until his vessel ceases to have any definite characteristics at all.[3] The solution often adopted, of making terms with the demands of charity by trusting " God's un-covenanted mercies " to save those who entrust themselves to the doubtful security of other vessels, somehow fails to commend itself to them as fulfilling the demands of charity, and has not hitherto noticeably promoted the cause of Christian reunion.

The whole situation is altered if we recognise that the

[1] On all this, see above, Essay V, iii.
[2] On all this, see Essay II.
[3] Compare the study of " Invincible Ignorance " in K. E. Kirk: *Ignorance, Faith and Conformity* (Longmans, Green & Co., 1925).

picture is based on a misunderstanding, on the acceptance as an integral element in the Christian faith of an error in the minds of men against which the Spirit of God has been striving down the ages. If the Church is to be regarded not primarily as an Ark of Salvation, but as the instrument of God's purpose, there is no inherent impossibility in the thought that what He needs is not a single vessel but a fleet. In that fleet there may be battleships, cruisers, submarines, supply ships and many another type of craft. The one thing there will not be is a ferry-boat, or any other kind of vessel devoted to passenger traffic; for where all are called upon to be members of the crew there is no need to make provisions for passengers.

Each vessel will then be justified in holding to the conditions required of those to be enrolled in its own complement. There will be no lack of charity if the crew of one ship, recognising that a man is not called by God for their type of service, advise him to enlist where God has need of him. But there is very serious lack of charity in that narrow-minded stupidity which imagines that God has need of only one type of vessel for His warfare against the world, the flesh and the devil, and in that pride which imagines one vessel alone to bear the brunt of the fight, and looks forward after victory to meet other crews with the words " *We* won the war."


### (f) *Summary*

The foregoing brief discussions may be summed up even more briefly, as follows :

1. In order that the full richness of the Christian way of life may be actualised on earth, it must be lived in more ways than any one individual or group can achieve.

2. The Christian doctrine of God inspires us to believe that human nature can be transformed so as to make this possible.

3. Christian reunion means nothing less than the binding together of all men in the brotherhood of one family, the brotherhood permeating every corner of life, yet preserving variety.

4. The present disunion of the Church is not merely the loss of a unity she once had : it is a stage in her striving towards a unity which has never yet existed on earth.

5. The Church is the body of Christ through which He works to achieve this unity. Corporately and individually her members are called to concentrate their minds on the glory of God and the achievement of His purpose, regarding their own salvation as, so to speak, a by-product of the process.

It will be seen that these five conclusions converge to describe a single point of view which underlies all that will be said in the remainder of this essay. Its adoption by no means provides a solution of the problems that lie before us, but it does provide, I believe, a standpoint from which they can be hopefully and profitably discussed. To aim at re-capturing a lost unity is a depressing ideal, and as unprofitable as all other attempts to roll back the course of history. But the thought of Christ's Church as His instrument in a creative work, looking forward down the ages to a future more glorious than the past or the present has seen, gives an inspiring ideal, for which it is worth while to think and act, to live and die. It is true that penitence for past sins, the effects of which now provide a serious part of our problems, must be interwoven in our outlook ; but Christian penitence never aims merely at unrolling the course of history and restoring the *status quo ante*. Atonement for the Christian is the putting forth of God's omnipotence to transform the results of sin into means for the furtherance of His purpose, and the penitent is encouraged to think of the " joy in heaven " which is caused by his restoration to the status of an effective " fellow-worker with God."

To aim at this ideal should breed in us a spirit of patience as we work at the problems which lie before us. We are to build for a glorious future, and must do our best to see that the foundations are well laid. On the side of a Yorkshire hill may be seen the beginnings of a magnificent church built by a religious community. The present members of that community have no expectation of seeing it completed in their lifetime, but that does not trouble them, for it is not built for their glory but to the glory of God, and God has

no need to hurry. " He that believeth shall not make haste."
It is in that spirit that I would offer some suggestions
concerning the problems presented to-day by a disunited
Christendom.

## II. THE ANGLICAN POSITION

In my youth I was trained in what may be called the
geographical theory of Church unity. According to that
theory Christ founded one Church to spread over the surface
of the earth. In each locality there could be only one society
representing that world-wide body. In England its true
representative was the Church of England ; in Italy, France
and Spain it was the Church of Rome. At the Reformation
the Church of England had preserved its catholic continuity
of faith and order, but had justifiably reformed itself by
refusing to recognise certain mistaken developments in
Western Christianity. In withdrawing his followers from
communion with the English bishops the Bishop of Rome
had formed them into a schismatic body which had no more
right to exist in England than a Church of England mission
in Italy. With this geographical theory of unity was
combined a strict doctrine of apostolic succession, and a
conviction that it was sinful either to add to or subtract from
the " faith once delivered to the saints " enshrined in the
Apostles', Nicene and " Athanasian " Creeds. Bodies which
had not been faithful to the threefold order, the apostolic
succession, and the three creeds, did not belong to the true
Church at all ; among those which had the world was divided
geographically.

This theory, like all theories based on undue simplification of history, has failed to stand the test of time. It might
conceivably suffice to justify the existence of his Church in
the eyes of a member of the Church of England who never
let his vision stray beyond the shores of his own country,
except to contemplate the Churches of the British dominions
beyond the seas. But what possible justification can it offer
for the existence of the Protestant Episcopal Church in the
United States of America, or of the Churches in China and
Japan which are in communion with the see of Canterbury ?

The question is not that of a local national church claiming to represent the one true Church in a certain corner of the earth : it is the question of a world-wide non-Roman Catholic communion containing in all probability members of every race, tongue and nation under the sun.

Of the historical tangle provided by the events of the Reformation, English and Continental, I do not propose to speak, having no competence to do so. I will only say that I believe my teachers to have been right in holding that the Church of England successfully preserved the apostolic succession and the faith of the early Church. But I do not believe that it is possible either to justify or discredit the present existence of a body by reference to obscure and disputed events in its past history. The kind of argument which would restore the Anglican communion to the Papal fold on the ground of technical errors in the process of separation four centuries ago, might equally well detach the southern states from the United States of America, restore the American colonies to their English allegiance, and place a descendant of the Jacobite line to rule over them all. Possibly all these causes have their adherents, who spend their time in trying to roll back the course of history whence it came. But surely what we have to do is to take the present situation as it comes down to us from the past. We need to know all we can of its history in order to understand its present conditions and its possibilities for the future. But no member of any church need be disturbed by finding that it did not originate as the work of well-informed and clear-sighted men acting from the single motive of doing God's revealed will. History does not move in that way, but in a tangle of mixed motives among all sorts and conditions of men. I will simply reaffirm my conviction that the underlying cause of the disruption of Christendom was that the centrifugal force of human unbrotherliness, brought to a head by the rise of national self-consciousness, proved for the time being too strong for the centripetal influence of Christ in His Church. Among the fragments into which that Church was broken was one which has grown to be this world-wide Church in communion with the see of Canterbury. What contribution has it to make to the Catholic Church of the future ? It is by the making of that contribution, not by the accident of its origin, that its history will be justified.

Stripped of detail and reduced to its essence, the Anglican position rests on the conviction that Christianity was from the beginning, and still is in God's intention, the religion of a corporate society. Christ did not leave behind Him a number of individual Christians who after a while decided that it would be a good thing to have an organisation and thus formed the Church. The original Church was the company gathered together in one place on the day of Pentecost, " on whom the Spirit came," and they went out and made other men Christians by baptising them into the fellowship of their society. The possibility of men and women living as Christians without being enrolled as members of the Christian society was an idea which did not belong to the first century ; it arose as a result of the Church's success in developing individual faith, and the problems it provides must be solved on their own merits in the age to which they belong.

For the Anglican, unity means unity vertically down the ages as well as horizontally across the face of the earth, unity with that little company in the Upper Room at Jerusalem as well as with fellow-Christians now alive in America, India and Japan. When an Anglican sets out to baptise a convert, he sets out to baptise him into that fellowship ; when the Anglican priest stands before the altar to celebrate the Holy Communion, or a lay-reader holds a mission service for half a dozen souls in some isolated region of Montana or Wyoming, that which is being done is an official act of the whole society functioning in that place. The members of a little gathering of twentieth-century Christians in an out-of-the-way corner of the world are to be assured that they are worshipping in communion with Peter and Andrew, James and John, the rest of that company, and the whole company of " just men made perfect " from that day to this.

This being his aim, the Anglican asks how that unity can be secured. He notices that in any earthly society unity and continuity from generation to generation seem to depend on two factors interwoven like two strands of a single rope : the outward continuity of organisation and the inward continuity of spirit, faith and practice. He notices, for example, that if a body of trustees are challenged as to their right to continue administering some endowment, they have to make good their position by showing both that they have been appointed constitutionally in accordance with the accepted custom of the trust, and that in their administration they are carrying out the intentions of the founder as he would like them to be carried out were he alive at the time. He concludes that he cannot rightly exercise less care in matters spiritual than is required in matters temporal, that he cannot offer to baptise into the fellowship of the Apostles if he is careless about either strand of the rope which links the Church of to-day to the Church of the Upper Room. Moreover, he would urge that it is a reasonable reading of history which finds empirical evidence that whenever attention is concentrated on one strand to the neglect of the other, true religion suffers in consequence. In so far as the Reformation was due to a much-needed moral protest, that protest was called for by an over-emphasis on the importance of the outward strand alone; and a similar one-sidedness in the Church of England in the eighteenth century made necessary the evangelical revival. Neglect of the outward strand has never been long persisted in without producing such fruits as the less desirable extravagances of Montanism, or careers such as that of Uriah Spragg.[1]

Holding these convictions, the Anglican finds himself bound to take seriously the question of Orders. If he is wise he does not rest his position on the belief that our Lord while on earth instituted a threefold order of Bishops, Priests and Deacons and left instructions for that to be continued down the ages. Not only is it impossible to discover positive historical evidence for that institution, but the probabilities are against it. The earliest Church was not concerned with forming an organisation to endure down the ages: it was looking for the soon-expected return of Christ to judgment. The Anglican is not surprised to find that there was at the outset an initial period in which the organisation of the Church

---

[1] See *The Strange Case of Miss Annie Spragg*, by Louis Bromfield (New York: Frederick A. Stokes, 1928). It seems more charitable in this case to refer to a novelist's representation of a type than to mention an historical character.

was in a somewhat fluid state, and to find evidence of differing types of organisation in different localities.    But as it became clear to the Church that it was to be an enduring society, and it settled down to its work, the organisation crystallised into the threefold order, with which we are familiar, as the standard form from the early second century to the sixteenth.    The Anglican sees no reason to doubt that in adopting this order the Church was guided by the Spirit of Christ according to His promise, and thinks that the burden of proof lies on those who would deny this rather than on those who accept it.

The question being whether or no the Church was right in holding this threefold order to express the mind of Christ, the answer cannot be found through an historical inquiry as to what the Church did then hold.    Once again we are driven to consider the question as a question of the present day. Approaching it in this way, the Anglican notices that by far the greater majority of Christians now alive still hold to the importance of the threefold order constitutionally appointed from generation to generation, and he concludes that if, in the Catholic Church of the future, due weight is to be given to the outward strand of the rope which binds the Church together down the ages, it will be by the preservation of this structure in the united body of Christ.

But within the Anglican communion there is not agreement as to the *theory* of what is the constitutional appointment of the ministry from generation to generation.    Two main types of theory can be distinguished.    According to one, the ministry is prior to the rest of the Church ; it is, as it were, the skeleton round which the body coheres.    According to the other, the Church-as-a-whole is prior to the ministry ; it is the body of Christ which concentrates its authority in certain members for the performance of certain functions as official acts of the whole.

If the Anglican communion could bring itself honestly to accept this latter theory as its official point of view, it would help to remove one of the most serious obstacles in the way of Christian unity.    For if the essence of orders is the concentration on the individual minister of the authority of the whole body of Christ, then with the shattering of that body has come a defectiveness in the orders of every Christian minister everywhere, be he Orthodox, Roman, Anglican or what not. Some communions have preserved the continuity of episcopal consecration, and others have not. But even in those which have, the authority concentrated upon the bishops officiating on each occasion is a defective authority, and the ministers of non-episcopal communions may be regarded as exercising the concentrated authority of that fragment of the body of Christ to which they belong. Given whole-hearted acceptance of this theory of orders, an agreement might be arrived at between an episcopal and a non-episcopal communion on the basis of mutual implementing of each other's already existent authority. The theory of orders first mentioned above drives the episcopalians to hold that in any such transaction they would do all the giving and the others all the receiving—an attitude of mind which effectually prevents any further progress in negotiations. On the second theory both give and both receive. Who gives and who receives most becomes a question of empirical fact to which God alone knows the answer and which it is unprofitable for man to ask.

Personally I believe this theory of orders to be the true one, and to give to any church which holds it full participation in the true catholic heritage. But it would be idle to pretend that it is *the* Anglican position. It has recently been advocated by Canon O. C. Quick,[1] and nothing is more to be desired than that it should be open-mindedly discussed up and down the Anglican communion. *Magna est veritas et praevalebit*, and when the truth has prevailed among us we shall be in a better position to move forwards towards unity.

Discussion of the Anglican position with reference to problems of reunion must of necessity be devoted mainly to the question of order. So far as the inward bond of faith and practice is concerned, there is less that need be said. The remarkable unanimity with which at Lausanne in 1927 the Nicene Creed was accepted as the basis of union in matters of faith, makes further discussion unnecessary at this point. The specific difficulty which the Anglican has to face is to

---

[1] See *The Christian Sacraments* (London: Nisbet & Co.; New York: Harpers, 1927), chap. vii. I am much indebted to Canon Quick's discussion for what I have written.

reconcile his conviction of the importance of the constitutionally preserved threefold order of the ministry as an essential element in the Catholic Church of the future with his recognition of the ministers of non-episcopal communions as ministering according to God's will during the period of disunion. If this difficulty can be overcome, those which remain can be discussed as arising, not out of the Anglican position in particular, but out of our attempt to evisage the Catholic Church of the Future.

### III. The Catholic Church of the Future

There are many definitions of the word "catholic." Whether what follows adds a new one, or draws out an element involved in those already in use, must be left to the reader to judge. The statement to be made is this. It is the essence of sectarianism to take some one element in the Christian way of life, or some one way of living it, treat it as though it were the whole, and require every member of the Church to live that way. It is the essence of catholicity to recognise that the full Christian life can only be lived by the Church as a whole, within which Church different individuals and groups must make their varying contributions to the richness of the common life.

Sectarianism is well illustrated by the story of a certain Scottish sect. Its essential obligation was strict observance of the rule in Acts xv. against eating "things strangled." Its adherents became divided on the question whether in buying a rabbit in a shop one was bound to satisfy oneself absolutely that it had been shot and not snared, or might charitably allow the vendor the benefit of the doubt. There was a strict party and a lax party, and the contention waxed so fierce between them that the sect split into two sects, each with a now more precisely defined *articulum stantis vel cadentis ecclesiae*. The lament of a pious adherent over the trouble caused by "they wearifu' rabbits" may provoke a smile, but the story is a parable with a serious interpretation. Whether the selected element be belief in justification by faith only or in transubstantiation, whether it be reliance on the "inner light" of the Society of Friends or on the technique of living expounded in "The First Century Christian Fellowship," whether it be the way of life of the Anglo-Catholic or of the Ulster Protestant or of the member of a confraternity of mystics—in these and all similar cases, for any one group to assert that its way of living the Christian life is the only true way is to repudiate the catholic ideal. This manner of procedure leads not to unity but to multiplication of sects, and incidentally gives rise to a great deal of unnecessary cruelty in the propagation of religion; for there are few things more cruel than to preach that a man ought to have a kind of experience which he is not destined by God to receive.

In contact with this a truly catholic church aims at encouraging the development within it of every conceivable genuine method of living out the Christian faith, and sternly forbids the exponents of any one way to arrogate to themselves a position of superiority over the rest. This is not always an easy task, and success is not always attained. There is a continual danger, for instance, of life within a religious order being thought a more perfect expression of Christianity than life in the world, and mystics are notoriously in need of submission to guidance by more ordinary Christians. Nevertheless it is a task to which any church must set itself if it is to be genuinely catholic, and its difficulties must be faced.

What kind of a unity can be sought for to harmonise the varieties of this polymorphous Christianity in one visible body on earth?

First let us ask what kind of a unity is required that all may recognise themselves as fellow-members of the one body. The answer is, surely, such unity as will make possible free intercommunion of all Christians at all altars of the Church catholic. This requires such unity as will make it possible for one churchman to recognise as his brother a fellow-member whose vocation is to live a very different kind of Christian life from his own, each needing the other's contribution to balance and complete his own in the corporate life of the Church. For this there is needed an agreed *order* such as will enable all without qualm of conscience to enter into their sacramental union with the Church of the ages, and an agreed *faith* such as will enable all to recognise one another's lives as fruits of the common tree of Christian devotion.

In the last section of this essay I have said all that I propose to say here on the subject of order : that in my belief the only kind of church order reasonably likely to meet our requirements is the historic order of the threefold ministry, and that the problem which lies before us is the problem of commending it so as to secure its acceptance in quarters where at present its importance is unrecognised. But lest it should be thought that to insist on this is to violate the principle of recognising the complementary value of polymorphous varieties of Christian living by ruling out non-episcopal forms of it, two things may be said here. First, we have to face the practical problem of enabling all to communicate together with a quiet conscience, and it is more reasonable to ask those who think episcopacy an unnecessary adjunct to Christianity to put up with it for the sake of the common good than to ask those who are honestly convinced of its necessity to abandon their convictions. Secondly, the acceptance of the threefold ministry and of episcopal ordination is *not* intended to connote the merging of other ways of Christian living in those customary within the present episcopal churches. It will demand of the episcopalians the recognition as their full brothers of fellow-Christians whose habits and customs are very different from their own, and may require an unprecedented divorce of administrative from sacramental authority. Of this more will be said later.

The question of *faith* presents difficulties of its own. At first one is tempted to say that what is required is an agreed minimum capable of expansion in differing directions. But for the reasons outlined above in the essay on " Authority," and at the beginning of this essay, the idea of a minimum is not satisfactory, and it is hard to know what else to suggest. That which unites different groups of Christians is not a lowest common denominator left behind after extracting the specific properties of each statement of it, but a transcendent reality too rich for embodiment in any one earthly form, gradually unfolding to man's apprehension further revelations of its inexhaustible splendour. The unity lies in the beyond, and is the source of our multiple apprehensions of it.  How then can we agree on a statement to unite us in our several apprehensions ?

Those who have read the earlier essays in this book will not be surprised at the statement that in my opinion the Church of Rome is right *in principle* in entrusting the duty of deciding what is and what is not of faith to a living body charged with the task of reconsidering the question from age to age.  In the ideal Catholic Church of the Future the question whether or no a particular development is or is not a genuine embodiment of Christianity will be decided, I believe, by its power of approving itself as such to the mind of the whole, and the Church will have to have a specialised organ of living members to consider the questions of this kind which will arise.  Unfortunately, in the Roman communion the body charged with this duty has nullified the soundness of the principle to which it owes its existence by in practice consistently repudiating the catholic in favour of the sectarian ideal, and it will be a long time before the principle recovers sufficiently from the discredit thus cast upon it for it to be accepted widely in other parts of Christendom.  It may even be submerged for a while in the Church of Rome itself, when that Church wakes up to what has been happening.

Moreover, what is required is not merely a board of reference to which developments of Christian apprehension may be referred after they have been made.  We are looking for an agreed point from which to start on our several explorations of the Christian way of life.  Perhaps this thought may suggest a better idea than " minimum " : it is an agreed starting-point or spring-board that we need.  Where is this to be found ?

Christianity began as the religion of a little band of men and women united by their common devotion to their risen Lord.  That devotion led them to worship Him as God, to recognise the working of God in the reception of the Spirit, and on the basis of this experience to transform their conception of God into the doctrine of the Trinity.  The foundation of it all was the acceptance of Jesus of Nazareth as one to be followed and worshipped as God.  Inexhaustible as are the riches of God's nature yet to be revealed to us, He has given us the starting-point for our quest of Him by making Himself known to us in flesh and blood. Acceptance of this starting-point is, I believe, what should be expected of all who are to be enrolled as members of Christ's Church. Moreover, it is religious belief rather than appreciation of the philosophical principles involved in it that should be expected, willingness to sing " Once in royal David's city " rather than to sign the Definition of Chalcedon.

What is the relation of this " starting-point " to the Apostles' and Nicene Creeds ? They are, surely, somewhat wordy statements of that very " starting-point," hammered out by the Church in order to preserve it inviolate through the controversies of the first four centuries of her life. If they are not that, they have no claim to our consideration ; if they are that they may rightly be repeated by all Christians as intending to express the faith of the Company of the Upper Room, though expressing it in a somewhat unfortunate mixture of religious and philosophical language unavoidable at the time of their composition. They are not final compilations of all that may or should be believed by every Christian ; nor (when regarded as starting-points) is repetition of them to be taken as implying belief in every detailed statement they contain. They have long stood as the Church's standard method of expressing what the Apostles believed. It should be made clear that they are put forward as expressing this, and as expecting the member of the Church to take his stand alongside St. Peter and St. John. If he is willing to do this, he is not to be troubled to answer questions directed to discovering whether he agrees in detail with the Church Fathers of the Fourth Century in their understanding of what was the content of the Apostles' Faith.

I count myself fortunate that I belong to a communion whose position on this matter is clearly and unequivocally expressed in its printed formularies. In the Book of Common Prayer of the Church of England the baptised child is required to be confirmed in order to be admitted to communion. In order to be confirmed he is required to learn the Catechism. In this he learns to say the Apostles' Creed, and then the official manual of instruction proceeds as follows :

*Question :* What dost thou chiefly learn in these Articles of thy Belief ?

*Answer :* First, I learn to believe in God the Father, who hath made me, and all the world.

Secondly, in God the Son, who hath redeemed me, and all mankind.

Thirdly, in God the Holy Ghost, who sanctifieth me, and all the elect people of God.

Men and women may be *encouraged* to fill out these statements, and expand them in many directions.    But no bishop or priest of the Church of England has a right to *demand* of any individual any fuller statement of his faith as a condition of admission to communion than that laid down in the official manual for the churchman's education.    This is as it should be, and is one of the marks of the intention of the Church of England to be true to the ideal of catholicity.

At the risk of revealing myself as hopelessly prejudiced, I must confess that to my mind the Anglican communion exhibits many of the marks of true catholicity.    I have spoken of catholicity as demanding such agreement in matters of faith and order as will enable exponents of different types of Christian living to communicate at the same altars.    That is what we find in the Anglican communion.    A single town may contain two or more churches of very different types of churchmanship, each with its own congregation at home in its own way of worship and life.    On a stormy winter's morning there is nothing to prevent the member of one congregation making his communion at the altar of the very different type of church which is hard by his residence, and this is often done.    What makes it possible ?    A common agreement to recognise the ministry of men ordained according to historic traditions of Christendom, and to say together the historic creeds without inquiring too closely of one another into what each means by them.

There is here most clearly illustrated the importance of attending to religious beliefs rather than to their implied philosophy when aiming at united worship.    To refer once again to the Catechism of the Church of England, the question " What is required of them who come to the Lord's Supper ? " is answered " To examine themselves, whether they repent them truly of their former sins, stedfastly purposing to lead a new life ; have a lively faith in God's mercy through Christ, with a thankful remembrance of His death ; and be in charity with all men." The " faith " which is required is not faith in this or that theory of the eucharistic presence. It is faith in the Living Lord whom the worshipper comes to meet, and it is as natural, possible and reasonable for two persons to come together to meet Him while differing in their ideas about the mode of His presence as it is for a subjective idealist and a realist to answer the same summons of a dinner-bell.[1] Only on the basis of a shared experience of hearing the bell can the two philosophers profitably begin to discuss the theory of it, and only on the basis of a shared devotion can two Christians profitably discuss its theology. The truth of this is well brought out by Canon Lilley's recent study of historic sacramental theory,[2] and the recent discussion between Canon Quick and the Master of Corpus Christi College, Cambridge, is further evidence of it.[3] To say that no church can be truly one without an agreed doctrine of the mode of Christ's sacramental presence [4] is about as mistaken a statement as it is possible to make. It is the duty of the Church to obey its Lord's command to " do this in remembrance of me," and to do so in such a way that all its members may be encouraged to come and find Him in the breaking of the bread. But a catholic church will avoid the sectarian tendency to assert that this cannot be done without accepting a certain theory of how He makes Himself known. It will welcome discussions of this mystery among its members as evidence that a common conviction of His presence among them makes the manner of it a matter of interest.

The unity at which we are to aim is a unity which will provide an agreed faith and order sufficient to form a starting-point from which men and groups of men in full intercommunion with one another may set forth to explore to the full the possibilities of the Christian life on earth. If this be so, then it is possible that the way to achieve it may be different from what is sometimes supposed. It is here that the

---

[1] See above, Essay IX, p. 103.
[2] A. L. Lilley: *Sacraments* (New York, 1929).
[3] See the issues of *Theology* (S.P.C.K.) for Jan., Feb., March and May 1929.
[4] Cp. Lord Halifax in Calvet, *Rome and Reunion* (London, 1928), p. ix.

distinction between sacramental and administrative authority, mentioned above, becomes of importance. Let us suppose that the Anglican communion had arrived at agreement with some non-episcopal communion to unite on the basis of (i) immediate mutual implementing of one another's already existing orders, (ii) an agreed method of ordination for the future, and (iii) an agreed acceptance of the Apostles' and Nicene Creeds as the starting-point for the life of faith in the united Church. The first step, and the only immediately essential one, would be the mutual implementing of orders. When that is done, there is no immediate necessity to fuse the administrative bodies. In England, for instance, the National Assembly of the Church of England and whatever corresponds to it in the other communion could continue to function side by side. No doubt liaison officers would be appointed to keep them in touch with one another, and gradually there would be worked out a less cumbersome administrative machinery for the united Church, during which process such questions as that of an agreed standard of educational attainments to be required of candidates for orders could be attended to. But this need not be hurried, and should be clearly recognised as a consequence of the union already effected, not as constituting the union itself. Similarly, in a town or village the already existing churches of each denomination would for the time being continue to function as before. The only immediate change would be that the members of each would be free if they wished, without fear of conscience or ecclesiastical censure, to have the interesting experience of " visiting around " at each other's altars. As time went on it might become clear that there were more churches in the neighbourhood than were required, and by an agreed scheme the number might be reduced. Again, this would be a consequence of the union already effected and not the actual method of union itself.

There is no more deadly enemy of aspirations after true unity than the temptation to find the ground of our need of unity in the economic wastefulness of overlapping centres of Christian work in given areas. Where this obtains it is a consequence of our present disunion, and its cure must be a consequence of union, not the method of it. It is a symptom and not a cause.   The ground of our need of unity is the fact that the body of Christ has been rent by human sin, and that He wills us to live and work together in brotherhood to the glory of God and for the good of mankind.   We must keep our eyes fixed firmly on this ideal of common worship and service in His body.   This alone will keep our policy of comprehensive catholicity from being a policy of weak compromise born of a lack of any definite convictions. It must be a policy based on the positive conviction that unity expresses itself in multiplicity, inspired by our doctrine of God to believe that human social life can be transformed after the image of the divine social life of the Blessed Trinity.

## IV. The Next Steps

If there is any truth in the main contentions put forward in this essay, the first step to be taken towards unity is steady and continued education.   The chief obstacle to be overcome is that natural unbrotherliness which has broken up the Church and now hinders its repair.   If anyone doubts this, let him ask himself how far in any department of life we have really learned to love our neighbours as ourselves. How many of us, for example, when we buy anything, really in our heart of hearts care as much that the seller gets a fair price as that we get good value for money?   How many manufacturers of motor cars, contemplating the prosperity of rival firms, rejoice as though the prosperity were their own, and thank God for the interesting conversation made possible among the confraternity of car owners by the variety of types they own?   How many a patriot really wants to see other nations remain themselves and prosper equally with his own, in order that each may make its own distinctive contribution to the welfare of mankind?   Illustrations could be multiplied *ad nauseam*;  these three should be enough to remind us that the chief obstacle to peace and brotherhood in every sphere of life is the difficulty that each and every one of us finds in conquering himself so as to appreciate persons unlike himself, and to wish them to continue and prosper in their unlikeness, because they can fill up what would be lacking in God's family if all were like himself.   Christ shows us the way to this in teaching that only by loving God the Father can we come to share His love for our neighbours. The moral of this for our purpose is that only by steadily looking away from ourselves to the vision of God's world-wide brotherhood of mankind can we counterbalance our tendency to rationalise our prejudices into irremovable obstacles in the way of its attainment.

It is probably impossible to overestimate the value of the educational work which has been done in England by the Student Christian Movement. Its temporary working principle of so-called " interdenominationalism," according to which it encourages its members to be loyal members of their own denominations in order that they may be loyal members of the Movement, has provided just the training needed. But there is still much to be done ; and, if I am not mistaken, the vastness of the area to be covered in the United States of America, and the failure of the Student Movement so far to take root and grow there as in England, have combined to make the grasping of this principle a slower process there. A parish priest is still too often hampered either by the expectation of his parishioners that he should rejoice to see his congregation grow at the expense of neighbouring denominations, or by the bland statement that there is no need to be loyal to any particular church since " all are going the same way." Over and over again he has patiently to explain that, although all are going to the same place, the individual will never get there at all unless he goes by some particular road which enables him to make progress along the pilgrim way.

In a girls' school known to me in New York excellent work is being done in international education among children of six or seven years old. An ingenious author devised the scheme of weaving stories around twins of various lands, and these books—" The Dutch Twins," " The Japanese Twins," " The Italian Twins," and the rest—are used as the school reading books, to the great interest of the girls. When a similar series of books about " The Roman Catholic Twins," " The Baptist Twins," " The Quaker Twins," and others form part of the regular curriculum of our Sunday Schools we shall have taken the first step towards unity.

We must learn to know, appreciate and love those with whom we are out of communion as the preliminary stage to finding our way to communion with them.

This must also be made a matter of prayer. There is a certain type of mind which, blind to the evidence of God's love of variety, is obsessed by the thought that He has ordained one mode of worship which alone is pleasing to Him. The first step, surely, is to love those who worship differently enough to long for their mistakes to be overlooked and their offering accepted. At the close of every service it is a common practice for each worshipper privately to ask God to accept his worship and pardon its faults and failings. A regular habit of combining with this a prayer for the acceptance of the service of all who try to worship Him, whatever their mode of worship, is one that might well be encouraged.

After education comes a step which has been already mentioned—the thorough study of the question of orders, with a view to discovering whether such suggestions as those of Canon Quick offer a possible line of advance. A word may perhaps be said here concerning the fears which some persons may feel lest to proceed on these lines in independence of the Church of Rome may bar the door for ever in the face of ultimate union with that Church. While we must never forget that no scheme in which Rome is not given a place can possibly be adequate, we may rightly, I believe, attempt to distinguish between such genuine demands of true catholicity which Rome has a right to expect to be preserved, and any inessential accompaniments of traditional practice which possibly both Rome and ourselves have mistakenly regarded as essential. The study of Canon Quick's suggestions is needed to enable us to arrive at a decision on the question whether or no they can be accepted without loss of a true continuity of catholic order down the ages. If it is found that they can, then we are justified in going ahead on them, in the faith that when Rome wakes up to discover that she is not the only pebble on the catholic beach she too will find out the truth of what has been revealed to us.

The vexed question of intercommunion must now be

mentioned.   From what has been said already it follows that intercommunion is the goal at which we aim, not the first step towards its attainment.   *Intercommunion is unity* ;  and the steps towards it are the findings of ways to such agreement on faith and order as make it possible for all without qualm of conscience.   To initiate immediate intercommunion as though these preliminary steps were unnecessary is like allowing a deep wound to heal over on the surface when its cure requires it to fill up with healthy tissue from within outwards.   The question when the skin may be allowed to grow over the wound is an empirical question to be decided by the doctor in charge of the case, and the nurse who works under him must wait for his word before this step is taken. In the life of the Church the local minister is the nurse, and it is not for him to decide whether the relations between his communion and another are such as to justify inter-communion within them.   It may be hard and painful for him to refrain from taking this step, but that is as it should be.   Disunity should be painful ;  but the pain should be welcomed as a spur to drive us on towards its healing, not succumbed to as a temptation to conceal it.   We should be waiting for the day when the message comes to tell us that terms have been arranged and we may invite our separated brethren to join with us at God's altar.

So much for the question of intercommunion in general, and of general invitations made locally to all and sundry to communicate at the same altar.   But I do not see why loyalty to this general rule should preclude provision being made for exceptions during the intervening period until unity be achieved.   It is much to be desired that the Anglican com-munion should establish in each diocese an authority charged with the power of granting dispensations of this kind, so as to permit, for example, the husband and wife of a mixed marriage to communicate together on the anniversary of their wedding day, or the members of a suitable joint conference to share in a corporate communion.

The study of the history of the Book of Common Prayer shows clearly to my mind that the rubric enjoining confirma-tion or the desire to be confirmed as a necessary condition of communion cannot rightly be interpreted as referring to the question of a desire to communicate on the part of a communicant member in good standing of another denomination. It is not because of that rubric in particular, but because the two bodies are " out of communion " in general that the priest's hands are tied.

Moreover, while the local priest should not issue invitations to intercommunion, the writings of such scholars as Canon T. A. Lacey and Dr. K. E. Kirk show that his right to refuse communion to those who present themselves on their own responsibility is, according to catholic tradition, far more limited than we often suppose, that a purely Anglican rigidity is often mistaken for a catholic principle. Even without the provision of the suggested dispensing authority the clash between the apparent claims of charity and loyalty to the general rule against intercommunion need not be so great as it is sometimes represented to be, or magnified into being.

Mention of this suggested dispensing authority reminds us of another desideratum of the Church, a commission charged with the duty of deciding what are and what are not genuine expressions of the Christian way of life, such as can be recognised as complementary members of the Catholic Church of the future. One advantage of abandoning the " Ark Theory " of the Church is that it is no longer necessary unduly to stretch the limits of the Church to include all men of good will, in order to avoid consigning them to perdition on account of their mistaken opinions. We can fully grant that men may be genuinely called by God to serve Him in other ways than as members of His Church,[1] and concentrate our attention on deciding what vessels can and what cannot be enrolled as members of God's fleet on active service. Extremely difficult empirical questions arise. Could the Society of Friends be admitted as a kind of religious order, bearing continuous and valuable testimony to the truth that sacraments are instruments of communion with God and not the communion itself?[2] What of Unitarians and Christian Scientists? Surely one of the first steps to be taken is a serious study of these questions in every communion which is looking forward towards the unity of Christendom.

[1] Cp. my *And Was Made Man*, p. 104.    [2] See above, Essay IX, p. 112.

Meanwhile, wherever it is possible for bodies to unite without compromise of principle on faith and order, the sooner they do so the better. I have in mind a small village in America where the population had declined until it was roughly true to say that the same congregation worshipped in the Presbyterian church in the morning, in the Baptist church in the afternoon, and in the Methodist church at night. The decision to close two of the buildings, and unite to worship under the leadership of one minister instead of three, found, apparently, no obstacles in convictions on either faith or order. The union was effected—so far as I can see, justifiably and successfully. There is at present a great deal of confusion owing to the persistence of divisions based on differences of conviction once held firmly, but now almost forgotten. Such unions as that just described help to dispel this confusion, and make it possible to see more clearly the real difficulties that have to be tackled.

There is no need to say anything here about that co-operation in every way possible in philanthropic, educational, social, international and missionary effort, which everyone recognises to-day as obligatory on Christians of differing denominations. This essay is already too long, although I have tried to confine it to putting together such suggestions as in my conceit and ignorance I believe not to be combined in this particular mixture elsewhere. The adage about fools rushing in where angels fear to tread is perhaps nowhere more often illustrated than in the readiness of academic persons to instruct those charged with adminis-trative duties in the conduct of their affairs. Quite possibly I am better occupied in theoretical discussions of freedom and providence than in making suggestions concerning the polity of the Church. But as it is my attempts to reflect upon freedom and providence which have issued in the thoughts about church unity which I have tried here to express, I have ventured to append them for what they are worth. It may be that the bearing of those previous observations will become clearer when viewed in the light of their application.

M

# XII. *CORRUPTIO OPTIMI PESSIMA*

## I

A FEW years ago an able student in one of our English theological colleges complained that, whenever he went to ask members of the staff about his intellectual difficulties, he always received the same reply : " Yes, that is a very interesting question. . . . It is a very difficult question. . . . Suppose we go and pray about it." A few years later, across the Atlantic Ocean and as far further as it takes to enter the realms of fiction, one Elmer Gantry at a Baptist seminary was similarly baffled by being told to take his difficulties to the Lord in prayer. It is clear that in both cases prayer was regarded (at any rate by the student) as an evasive substitute for thinking. But what is thinking ? And how does it differ from praying ? How do two men sitting down and discussing a problem over their pipes differ from those same two men kneeling to pray about it ?

If prayer is to be used as an evasive substitute for thinking, it must be with one of two ends in view : Either (*a*) the result of praying must be to divert attention from a troublesome problem, so that the thinker ceases to be interested in it, or (*b*) prayer must be a method of discovering the solution of a problem by which one may steal a march on those who follow the ordinary processes of thought. Neither of these notions is tenable, but the second of them may be used as the starting-point of our inquiry. In order to discuss it we must first ask what are the " ordinary processes of thinking " which the prayer is to beat at their own game.

There would be no thinking if there were nothing to think about, and there would be no point in thinking if there were nothing worth while thinking about. It is the object of the thought which determines the value of the thinking, and, in any purely intellectual quest, what we aim at is an apprehension of reality as it is. When two persons unite in such a quest, their aim is to share in apprehending a common object. Each will see it from his own point of view, but unless there be a common " it "—unless, indeed, there be an " it " which is not only common but recognisably common— their quest is a waste of time. Thinking is not a mental process carried on in abstraction from reality, which may or may not be " logical," for " logic " is in things before it is in human thought, and thinking is logical when it accurately apprehends what it thinks about. The thinker's aim is to know, and our processes of thinking are our ways of learning. Behind each one of us there is a long spatio-temporal history issuing in a unique being learning to know from his own point of view. Our mental vision is imperfect, but improving, and by combined effort in argument and discussion we can help to clear away the scales from one another's eyes. Thus we become the sort of people who can see what we could not see before.

That human life is a process of becoming the sort of people that we were not before is a truth too often overlooked in considering our mental activity. Let us imagine a man standing on the up-town platform of the Twenty-third Street Station of the Seventh Avenue Subway in New York. As a train comes in, he says " Here's a Broadway train." " How do you know ? " asks his companion. " By the two white lights," he replies. Now, once upon a time he has undoubtedly learned that two white lights mean a Broadway train, and has had to go through a process of thinking of the type : " Here are two white lights ; two white lights mean a Broadway train ; therefore this is a Broadway train." But he has now got beyond that stage. He is the sort of man who can recognise a Broadway train, and if a companion asks him how he knows it, he unrolls from the latter end the process by which he learned it : " How do I know that this is a Broadway train ? I know that this is a Broadway train because it has two white lights, and two white lights mean a Broadway train."

There are doubtless some people who would suggest

that as the train comes into the station his " unconscious "
once again goes through the process by which he has learned
to recognise Broadway trains, and communicates the result
to " his conscious mind." The suggestion is an imaginary
elaboration of events in an unverifiable field, based on the
premiss that whenever a truth has been learned through a
process of inference, it can never afterwards be recognised
except by a repetition of the process. On what grounds this
premiss rests, I am unable to discover; it goes beyond the
evidence and is inherently absurd. The evidence shows that
what we have learned by inference we can recognise directly,
and there is an inherent absurdity in a theory which involves
our maintaining that whenever a man meets his wife he
recognises her by a process of inference.

Moreover, the evidence of our experience shows that the
process of inference is itself built up of a series of direct
observations. The friend who first initiated us into the
mysteries of subway travel did so by sharing with us his
knowledge of three interconnected facts forming a complex
whole. We had to learn them *seriatim* in the process of our
development; but having learned them we become the sort
of man who can recognise Broadway trains at sight, and we
have no need to repeat the process of learning except for the
purpose of instructing someone else. If the facts are there
to be learned, and we are capable of learning them, then by
doing so we become what we were not before. I do not
see that we can get behind this statement; we must take it
as our starting-point in trying to understand human thinking.
In the spatio-temporal process human beings are creatures
capable of learning what they did not know before, and by
so doing they develop themselves into being what they were
not before. The hypothesis of " unconscious inference,"
and the theory of pre-natal memory in Plato's " Meno," seem
to be parallel attempts to get behind this starting-point,
both rendered unnecessary by " taking time seriously " and
recognising man's place in the process of creation.

Trains and wives are clearly objects about which we
think. We may apprehend them rightly or wrongly, but
we can only do so in virtue of their prior existence as material
for apprehension. The same is true of the meaning of the

white lights on the train. It is not an object of sense-perception; it may rightly be included among what some thinkers call "the imponderables," for such a meaning has no weight or other quality measurable by the use of scientific instruments. The same, again, is true of every argument or statement put forward in this essay. They are parts of my thinking, but only in the sense that they are the nature of reality as apprehended or misapprehended by me. If they are misapprehensions, there is only one way in which they can be corrected: I must learn more, so as to apprehend more clearly. This may come through having my eyes opened by some reader whose clearer apprehension enables him to show me what I have not seen.

Objectivity, the El Dorado of philosophers, is, in every direction of human inquiry, sought by faith rather than demonstrably exhibited as already found. In all our apprehensions up to date the element of subjective misapprehension is so inextricably intertwined with what is true that it is always easy for the epistemological sceptic to make out a plausible case for the denial of all objectivity in human thought. But still men go on seeking, discussing, and arguing, for we are human in virtue of our faith that there is something to be found, and we cannot cease to behave like human beings. In theism the act of faith which inspires all human thinking becomes aware of its own nature, and devotion to "the as yet partially apprehended objective" believes itself to be devotion to God revealing Himself through His creation and in the personal intercourse of religion.

When, therefore, two men sit down together to think out a problem, they are brother learners trying to discover more of the common reality which both desire to know. It may be that the past history of each has led to two such different points of view that in their present condition there is a violent clash of opinions, and the discussion proceeds by way of furious argument. But what gives point to the argument is the underlying faith that sooner or later they will be able to apprehend the common object of their search, and to see how it has come about that they have entertained such different notions of it.

If the theist be right in his conviction that God reveals

Himself both in the objective order of reality as discovered by human thought, and also in the personal intercourse of religion, then to seek communion with God in prayer need not be an evasion of the duty of thinking. But neither should it be regarded as a substitute for it. For him the duty of thinking is grounded in the conviction that it is God's will that he should learn by mental seeking, and the unquenchable faith which drives men onwards in the search is a seed sown by God in His creation of man, evidence of the divine intention that he should think. It is a common experience of teachers to have to withhold information which might be given to pupils,' in order that they may " make it their own " by finding it out for themselves, and the wise pupil will not try to evade his duty by cajoling his master into doing his work for him. Similarly the wise Christian will not try to evade his duty of thinking by turning to prayer. The knowledge of God gained by personal intercourse may, indeed, help him by illuminating his problems, and sharpening his wits ; but it will only do so if what he asks for is help to do his work better, and not an excuse for abandoning the task.

The advice to pray may be either a recommendation to take steps towards girding up the loins of the mind, or a mistaken counsel to seek to evade the doing of God's will. Which of these two it is can only be determined in each particular case as it arises. If it be the former, it is the best advice that can be given ; if the latter, the worst. The latter is a kind of caricature of the former, the degradation of prayer into an instrument not for doing, but for thwarting God's will. Which it actually was in the two cases mentioned at the beginning of this essay, is not in question here. If the critical English student and Mr. Sinclair Lewis were right in suspecting the worst, they were right, too, in their scorn of it. But the scorn was deserved for a reason they did not give. It was deserved because they were each confronted with a case of *corruptio optimi pessima*.

## II

It is a curious truth that profound belief in objectivity often appears at first sight indistinguishable from reliance on the highest degree of subjectivity in thinking. It is worth while to observe how this comes about. If the aim of our thought is to apprehend objective reality, then the end of every search must be an act of apprehension. The only way in which one explorer can communicate what he has found to another is by describing it, or pointing it out. To use Professor Dewey's term, his method is denotative. " This," he says in effect, " is the truth as I see it; cannot you see it for yourself? " If the other man can and does so see it, then all is well. But if not, then how is his friend to convince him that what he described is indeed the truth and not his erroneous misconception of it, seeing that the word " truth " must always be qualified by the phrase " as I see it " ?

It may be, of course, that he is wrong. But let us assume for the sake of argument that he is right. What can he do ? We have seen that the objectivity in which he believes includes the relations whereby all the elements of reality are linked together in a complex intelligible whole. A " logical " argument is a progressive series of apprehensions of truly existent relations. The whole network of relations is so complex, and the problems involved in trying to apprehend them are so confusing, that it is often extremely difficult, if not beyond our powers, to select and observe accurately those relevant to a particular inquiry. But there is no other way of proceeding, and when two explorers disagree, what they have to do is to find some common starting-point from which they may again set out on the voyage of discovery. To go back to our problem. If a man has rightly apprehended the nature of $x$, but cannot bring his friend to see it, then his next step will be to say " At any rate you agree with me as to the nature of $a$; then can't you see that if $a$ is such, $b$ must be so and so ? " and so on. At any point in the journey from $a$ to $x$ there may be disagreement, and it may be necessary to turn aside and unravel that. The process is apparently endless, and life is all too short for an individual to experience the unravelling of more than a few disagreements.

Moreover, we continue to grow in our awareness of the complexity of the problems before us—as witness those presented by investigations in the worlds of physics and astro-physics. In philosophy, perfect work waits upon patience.

There is always the appearance of subjectivity because every statement, true or false, is a pointing out of " the truth *as I see it*." There is no criterion of general application whereby we may eliminate the element of subjectivity, and thus distinguish the true from the false. There are many expedients which can be used as guide-posts in our journeys of discovery ; nearly every branch of study develops its own canons in the course of its work, and a general sense of direction is provided by our faith in an all-pervasive rationality which forbids us to rest content with unresolved contradictions. But in the last resort, discovery of the truth can only be said to come by acts of apprehension, through a kind of insight which is inexplicable in terms of anything else, but familiar to every human being through his own experience of it. A man may not be able to apprehend the solution of the problems to which an Einstein applies himself, but he can tell a penny stamp from a halfpenny one, and recognise his wife in a crowd.

As a result of these facts, the inquirer has often to face two difficulties, which need to be understood. In the first place, our desire for objective certainty tempts us to allow the wish to become the father to the thought, and to believe that we can achieve some infallibility free from the limitations of subjective apprehension. Because it is easy to forget that every argument is a series of such apprehensions, each subject to the same limitation, it is easy to imagine that a lengthy argument gives a greater guarantee of objectivity than a single act of apprehension. This danger is at its greatest when we are dealing with certain elements in reality which are indefinable in terms of anything other than themselves, such as freedom, obligation, and that power of apprehension which is the subject of our present inquiry. It is often easier to make a plausible argument explaining away these realities, and describing them as something other than their true selves, than to win conviction by leading a man consciously to apprehend them as they actually exist in his experience. It seems weak to go on reiterating " This is so ; cannot you see it ? " in the face of apparently profound and learned arguments showing deep insight into the nature of almost every subject except the one under discussion. In such a case, all that can be done is to bring negative criticism to bear on the proposed substitutes for freedom or obligation, or whatever else it may be that is in dispute, showing that the suggested theory breaks down when applied to some experience admittedly apprehended alike by both parties to the inquiry, and that somewhere in the course of the argument by which it has been maintained there is a step which can only be justified by a reiteration similar to one's own. When this has been done, one's own reiteration does not sound so weak as before.

The second difficulty arising out of the reduction of all argument to the statement of subjective apprehensions is this. If this is all that can be done, we may feel, why should we prefer one man's statement to another ? If all argument is of the nature of the street urchin's form of controversy, a repetition *ad nauseam* of " 'Tis ! " and " 'Tisn't ! " what is the use of arguing at all ? All we have are differing subjective opinions, any one of which is as likely to be true as another.

But there is an element of perverseness in this scepticism which betokens a radical weakness in philosophical education. It is perhaps natural for the student of philosophy to pass through a stage in which the interest of view-tasting temporarily obscures that passionate desire for the truth which gives birth to the true philosopher. To allow the student to become fixed at this stage, and to produce view-tasters rather than genuine seekers for truth, is, in the field of philosophical education, the *corruptio optimi pessima* which needs to be most carefully guarded against. The view-taster may be a promising student, but it is the mark of maturity to have passed beyond that stage, and to be once again a devotee of truth. To adapt the words of the Epistle to the Hebrews, he that will come to the knowledge of reality must believe that reality is, and generously rewards those who earnestly seek it.[1]

[1] Heb. xi. 6.

Given this devotion and this faith, a man begins to discover that he will be foolish if he refuses to acknowledge that the insight of all men is not equally valuable on every subject. He will admit that as a general rule a medical training makes a man more likely to diagnose correctly a case of sickness, and a mathematical training to solve a problem in mathematics. He will not think so poorly of the achievements of the human race as to deny that we have garnered some wisdom which may be of use to us in future inquiries. In the end he will conclude that the aim of education should be not so much the imparting of information already acquired, as the development of a pupil into the kind of man whose insight into the problems of his field of study is acute and trustworthy.

If this be so, then the bedrock on which we always have to fall back in our quest for knowledge is the insight of men specially qualified to deal with the kind of problem under discussion. When this fails, and " doctors differ," there is no external court of appeal; there is nothing to do but to gird up the loins of the mind for further patient seeking.

We are now approaching the point at which this essay has been aiming from the start, for it has had an aim through all its apparently inconsequent rambling. Our best achievements in the quest of knowledge are the records of their apprehensions made by men whose insight has led them aright; our worst are the utterances of those whose vision has led them astray—and there is no distinction of form whereby we can tell the one from the other. So far as the form of the statement is concerned, each is a dogmatic assertion of " the truth as I see it." Nevertheless, the one is the truth apprehended by man's only method of grasping it, and the other is a caricature of it; the one is the *optimum* in the use of our intellects, and the other its *pessima corruptio*. It is not by changing our method of thinking, but by changing ourselves so that we employ better the one and only method, that we may avoid error and discover truth. There is not one " logical method of thinking " which leads to truth, and another " illogical method of thinking " which leads to error; the same method which in its perfection finds truth in its corruption brings error.

I was led to these reflections by reading over the essay printed above under the title of " Compromise, Tension and Personality," and recalling to mind Sir Edmund Gosse's account of his father's attempt to reconcile his geological knowledge with his acceptance of the account of Creation in Genesis as literal history.[1]   His suggestion was described as implying that God had hidden the fossils in the rocks in order that in the fullness of time they might be a test of faith for nineteenth-century Christians.   It occurred to me that a critic might dismiss my contention as a twentieth-century version of the elder Gosse's position.   Nevertheless, despite the points of similarity between the two, I remain convinced that the one is a caricature of the other.   It has further occurred to me that in all probability there is no major contention put forward in this book which might not similarly be caricatured, and how can I, in every case, communicate my conviction that the one is an apprehension of truth and the other the caricature, and not *vice versa* ?

I cannot.   I can only attempt to state as honestly and clearly as possible " the truth as I see it," and appeal to my readers to join in the inquiry, asking them over and over again, " Cannot you see it for yourself ? "   The only stipulation I can make is that my critics shall join in the task as devotees of truth, and not as view-tasters.   Then by their criticism they will be able to help me to overcome the deficiencies of my own vision, and to revise my views where revision is required.   For what I need is to become the kind of man who can see better than I see now, and we can all help each other to transform ourselves, and to set forward the progress of human knowledge.   Meanwhile I continue to believe that the pursuit of philosophy will be helped and not hindered by combining with the habit of hard and accurate thinking the habit of " taking it to the Lord in prayer " ; and I hope that the grounds of this belief are sufficiently obvious from what I have already written.

[1] See *Father and Son* (London : William Heinemann, 1910), pp. 108–110.

# INDEX